D0428171

THE GR

THE GREEKS

An introduction to their culture

Robin Sowerby

London and New York

First published 1995
by Routledge
11 New Fetter Lane, London EC4P 4EE

Simultaneously published in the USA and Canada
by Routledge
29 West 35th Street, New York, NY 10001

© 1995 Robin Sowerby

Typeset in Baskerville by
J&L Composition Ltd, Filey, North Yorkshire
Printed and bound in Great Britain by
Biddles Ltd, Guildford and King's Lynn

British Library Cataloguing in Publication Data
A catalogue record for this book is available from the British Library

Library of Congress Cataloguing in Publication Data
A catalogue record for this book has been requested

ISBN 0–415–12041–1
0–415–12042-X (pbk)

CONTENTS

CONTENTS

FIGURES

PREFACE

What makes the Homeric poems a formative influence in western culture? What is distinctive about Greek drama? What are the main tendencies in the thought of Plato and Aristotle and how do the two philosophers differ? What is it about Greek art that has made it classical in the eyes of future time?

It is to help those enquiring into the Greek legacy for the first time to answer such questions as these that this book has been written. It concentrates on the mainstream flowing from Homer onwards. Since Homer had a shaping influence upon subsequent Greek culture, the first chapter not only introduces the *Iliad* and the *Odyssey* but also seeks to define the Hellenic spirit encapsulated in the poems and transmitted to posterity. The second chapter provides an outline history of the post-Homeric world within which there is a brief account of the growth of Athenian democracy, arguably the most radical development of the Greek *polis*, and the context of most of the cultural achievements that are treated in subsequent chapters on literature, philosophy and art. Concentrating on the most creative figures of the surviving legacy, the emphasis of the book, after the Homeric beginning, is necessarily Athenian and classical. At the same time there is an attempt to put the surviving legacy into a general cultural context. The historians, for example, are set against the history they were writing about. Developments in literature, philosophy and art are related to a wider picture and relations are made between them so that readers may form a synoptic view.

The book does not, therefore, offer a general survey of Greek life. Social, economic, religious and legal factors are not given the prominence that such a survey might require. Nor is there the intention to offer a general survey of all the great cultural achievements. Rather a series of representative texts and works of art is chosen which are in some way typical of what is distinctive and best in the cultural legacy. For example, there is no general survey of the plays of Sophocles; the needs of a first-time reader are perhaps better served by a more extended discussion of Sophocles' most famous play, *King Oedipus*, in relation to the classic account of drama in Aristotle's *Poetics*. There is also more quotation than would be usual in a general survey. The idea is to give new readers a brief experience of the text in the hope that they may be encouraged to explore further for themselves.

Modern translations are from the Penguin classics where these are available. Otherwise Loeb translations are used. A complete list is included at the end of the text. Classical references have long been standardised and are given in most editions and translations of the text. Classical names are given in the form in which they are most familiar in English. Dates are all BC unless otherwise stated. A chronological table is included for convenience at the end of the text.

1

THE HOMERIC POEMS

Unity of plot is not, as some think, achieved by writing about one man . . . Homer especially shows his superiority in taking a right view here – whether by art or nature.

Aristotle, Poetics, VIII

Though the classical era is traditionally regarded as beginning in the early fifth century, an account of Greek civilisation must begin with the Homeric poems, probably composed between two or three centuries earlier. The view that Homer 'had educated the Greeks' (*Republic*, X, 606) is a commonplace reported by Plato in the fourth century. His poetry was a central part of every Athenian schoolboy's education. Indeed the historian Xenophon, writing in the early fourth century, records the experience of a contemporary figure called Niceratus: 'My father in his anxiety to make me a good man made me learn the whole works of Homer; and I could now repeat by heart the entire *Iliad* and *Odyssey*' (*Symposium*, III, 5). As the classic expression of the Hellenic spirit, the Homeric poems had a formative influence upon the culture of later times, so that they are our natural starting point.

HOMER AND HISTORY

The special status of Homer in the Greek world is attested to in early Greek literary sources recording the existence of a guild called the Homeridae claiming to be the descendants of Homer who flourished in Chios and were devoted to the recitation of his poems. The more widespread existence of other professional reciters of Homer's poems called rhapsodes is also well attested. One such rhapsode called Ion features in the philosophical dialogue of Plato that bears his name. Nevertheless it may seem surprising that there is no consistent tradition about Homer (other than agreement on his name) in the later literature of Greece. Different views are recorded concerning his date and time. According to some accounts he had been a contemporary witness of the Trojan War; according to others the poems were composed sometime after the fall of Troy, an event which in any case was for the Greek historians shrouded in the mists of prehistory. In the absence of other literary evidence we are indebted to modern archaeologists, and especially to the pioneering work of Heinrich Schliemann (AD 1822–90), for material knowledge about the world of Homer's poems.

The island of Crete was the earliest centre of civilisation in the Mediterranean. The remains at Cnossos show that the Bronze Age civilisation called Minoan (from Minos, the mythical lawgiver of Crete) was highly developed and lasted from roughly 3000 to 1000 BC. On mainland Greece, a Bronze Age civilisation, centred upon royal palaces such as those excavated at Mycenae, Tiryns and Pylos, developed somewhat later and lasted from about 1580 to 1120. This civilisation is called Mycenaean after what seems to have been its most powerful centre, Mycenae. In Homer, Agamemnon, leader of the Greek expedition to Troy and most powerful of the Greek princes, comes from Mycenae which Homer calls 'rich in gold', 'broad-streeted' and 'well-built'. In the Catalogue of Ships in Book Two of the *Iliad*, believed by some to describe Greece as it was known in Mycenaean times, the largest numbers come from Mycenae and Pylos.

After the destruction of Cnossos in 1400, Mycenaean civilisation was at its most powerful and advanced. The most substantial remains at Mycenae, the so-called Treasury of Atreus and the Tomb of Clytemnestra (Atreus was the father of Agamemnon and Clytemnestra was his wife), were built after 1300 and the Lion Gate of Mycenae (so called from the relief over its lintel) dated from 1250. The fortification walls were mighty indeed. They were between 12 to 45 feet thick and it has been estimated they were as high as 40 feet. The treasures found by Schliemann in the royal graves at Mycenae which include the famous gold face masks, bear witness to the opulent beauty of Mycenaean artwork, which was highly sophisticated in craftsmanship and design. The golden

Figure 1   Mycenae (*photograph: Richard Stoneman*)

cup of Nestor (*Iliad* XI, 632–7) resembles an actual cup found in the graves at Mycenae. Another Mycenaean survival is the boar's tusk helmet of Odysseus (*Iliad* X, 261–5), which is of a kind

Figure 2   Mycenaean boar's tusk helmet (*photograph: Richard Stoneman*)

3

found in Mycenaean tombs and not found in later excavations. The techniques of engraving, enchasing and embossing were well developed and so was that of inlaying bronze with precious metals. Ivory and amber imported from the east and the north are commonly found and indicate the extent of Mycenaean commercial relations. Mycenaean pottery of this period is found widely throughout the Mediterranean, a further indication that the Mycenaeans were great sailors and traders.

Excavations at Hissarlik in northern Turkey, which Schliemann believed to be the site of Troy, have recorded nine settlements, the seventh of which was destroyed by a great fire in the mid-thirteenth century so that archaeological evidence seems to lend support to the possibility of an historical Trojan War of which the Homeric account records the poetic memory. Soon after the possible date for the sack of Troy, the great Mycenaean centres were themselves destroyed by the invasion of the Dorians from the north who initiated what is usually known as the Dark Ages, lasting from 1100 to 800. The Bronze Age gave way to the Iron Age. The main metal in Homer is bronze but there are iron weapons too. In fact there is a considerable historical mixture as the Homeric poems record practices and customs that differ from those of Mycenaean times.

Figure 3 Troy (*photograph: Richard Stoneman*)

For example, the Mycenaeans buried their dead, while in Homer the dead are cremated. Experts on warfare note that in the fighting described in *Iliad* XIII, 131–5, tactics are employed which imply the use of the phalanx, an organised line of hoplites (infantrymen) that did not come into being until the formation of the city state, possibly suggesting a date as late as 800. Some have thought the scenes of ordinary life depicted in the similes and on the shield of Achilles (including a glimpse thereon of a public trial before a jury of elders without reference to the king) are those of Homer's own day and that the poet is deliberately drawing parallels between a heroic past and a humble present, thereby bringing his material up to date. The Homeric poems are believed (largely on linguistic grounds) to have emanated from Ionia, so that they may have preserved the memory of the Mycenaean mother culture transmitted by those who had colonised Asia Minor in the dispersal that followed the Dorian invasion.

Linguists have identified the same kind of layered structure as that revealed by the archaeologists, in which archaic elements co-exist side by side with later forms. The language of Homer is a fusion of elements from various dialects, the chief of which are the Ionic, the Aeolic and the Arcadian. The Arcadian and Aeolic dialects are thought to have developed from dialects of Greek spoken in mainland Greece in the south and north respectively during the Mycenaean period. The fusion of these two dialects with the later Ionic (which is the predominant element) has contributed to the view that Ionic bards took over and adapted to new circumstances and a new audience material which they had inherited from the past. The oldest linguistic elements are probably what have come to be known as the 'traditional epithets' like 'cloud-gathering' Zeus, or 'ox-eyed' Hera, some of which perplexed the Greeks themselves. Their presence can be accounted for by the technique of formulaic composition employed in the poems. Formulae may be short phrases like 'winged words' or 'rosy-fingered dawn', or extend to longer passages describing repeated actions such as arming for battle, the preparation of a meal or the ritual of sacrifice. They are convenient units that can be readily committed to memory and are therefore an aid to improvisation in a pre-literate world where the poet is wholly dependent upon memory. About one-third of the lines in the poems is repeated wholly or in part in the course of the poem. Equally, one-third is made up of phrases and formulae that are not repeated elsewhere. It is clear that the traditional inheritance was constantly being added to, to meet contemporary needs and the requirements of different tales. In the twentieth century AD, the pioneering work of the American scholar Milman Parry showed how sophisticated is the deployment of the formulaic technique in Homer, and from a comparative study involving modern oral poets in the Balkans showed how this technique is fundamental to both the composition and transmission of oral poets. Homer's language therefore had been purposely developed for poetic recitation; it was never a spoken language. Nor did such a development any more than the tales themselves originate with one genius. There is a consensus of scholarly opinion that the language of the Homeric poems evolved over many centuries and that its sophisticated technique of formulaic diction goes back to the Mycenaean age, from which it was doubtless transmitted by practising bards like Demodocus and Phemius in the *Odyssey*.

And so the Homeric poems are a record of the heroic values of Mycenaean civilisation, an aristocratic culture based upon the great palace, of which the remains excavated by Schliemann at Mycenae are the physical example and the Ithacan home of Odysseus with its resident singer of tales is the poetic representation. They are generally regarded by most modern scholars as having been substantially composed long after the culture they describe had passed away, probably in the early or mid-eighth century.

THE *ILIAD*

In the *Iliad* the heroic aristocratic virtues are proved on the battlefield. Old Nestor reports that when he recruited Achilles for the Trojan expedition the latter's father Peleus had told his son 'always to excel and do better than the rest' (XI, 784). Speaking in battle to the Greek Diomedes, the Lycian Glaucus tells him that his father had given him the same instruction, telling him not to shame his forebears who were the best in Lycia (VI, 208–10). Hector's hope for his son Astyanax is that in future time men will say 'He is better than his father' as he returns from the battlefield bearing the bloodstained armour of his foe (VI, 479–81). The Homeric hero consciously endeavours to excel. No

6

distinction in this respect is made between Greek and Trojan for the Trojans are not seen as some inferior race of barbarians but are equally responsive to the heroic impulse. In fact Homer puts his fullest and most famous expression of it into the mouth of the Trojan ally Sarpedon (XII, 310–28). Here is the speech in the version of the eighteenth-century translator of Homer, Alexander Pope, who manages in his heroic couplets to capture something of its grand effect.

> 'Why boast we, Glaucus! our extended reign,
> Where Xanthus' streams enrich the Lycian plain,
> Our num'rous herds that range the fruitful field,
> And hills where vines their purple harvest yield,
> Our foaming bowls with purer nectar crowned,
> Our feasts enhanced with music's sprightly sound?
> Why on these shores are we with joy surveyed,
> Admired as heroes, and as gods obeyed?
> Unless great acts superior merit prove,
> And vindicate the bount'ous powers above.
> 'Tis ours, the dignity they give, to grace;
> The first in valour, as the first in place.
> That when with wond'ring eyes our martial bands
> Behold our deeds transcending our commands,
> Such, they may cry, deserve the sov'reign state,
> Whom those that envy, dare not imitate!
> Could all our care elude the gloomy grave,
> Which claims no less the fearful than the brave,
> For lust of fame I should not vainly dare
> In fighting fields, nor urge thy soul to war.
> But since, alas! ignoble age must come,
> Disease, and death's inexorable doom;
> The life which others pay, let us bestow,
> And give to fame what we to nature owe;
> Brave though we fall, and honoured if we live,
> Or let us glory gain, or glory give!'

Sarpedon asks Glaucus why they are singled out for honours at the feast, with special seats and the best food and drink among the Lycians, who look upon them as gods. Why do they have the best land with orchards and wheatfields? Their social position obliges them to lead the Lycians in fighting so that their followers will acknowledge that they earn their privileges by virtue of their great prowess on the battlefield. At the same time Sarpedon says that if they could actually be like gods and avoid old age and death, he would not urge Glaucus to join the fight where glory is gained. The Homeric adjective 'bringing glory' fits the context well. Elsewhere Homer uses many adjectives that express the grisliness of the fight. But since they cannot escape death in its countless forms, Sarpedon urges that they join the fight and either gain honour for themselves or give it to others.

The heroic resolve is the conscious choice to risk a glorious death rather than forgo glory for the sake of holding on to an insignificant life. Moreover the choice is made wholeheartedly. Homer has a word, *charma*, to express eagerness for battle and joy in the fight. Despite the foreboding he has of his own death, as he enters the fray Hector is likened to a stallion who has broken loose and is galloping off joyfully to his favourite pasture confident in his own splendour (XV, 263–8). Achilles is the supreme embodiment of the hero by virtue partly of the superior physical prowess that enables him to excel others in the fight but even more so by virtue of the choice he has made in being at Troy at all, for he reports that his goddess mother Thetis had told him that he could choose between two destinies: a long and undistinguished life if he returned home or eternal fame if he remained at Troy (IX, 410–16). Thetis herself later tells us that Zeus had allowed her to produce a child who would excel all heroes. We can imagine that the myth of Achilles as Homer inherited it was the supremely heroic myth: the greatest glory exacts the greatest price and Achilles is the supreme hero in making his heroic choice in full knowledge of its ultimate cost.

The anger of Achilles: the tragic pattern

But the celebration of the hero and of the Mycenaean culture which had fathered the myth is not the main subject of Homer's *Iliad*. The heroic choice is taken for granted and is of secondary significance; ironically, we only hear of it when Achilles is threatening to throw it away by going home. Homer's subject, announced in the very first word of the poem, is the anger of Achilles that brings ruin in its train. His heroic aspirations are threatened by a chain of events following on from the quarrel he has with Agamemnon in the opening book. In the ninth year of the siege of Troy, the god Apollo is angry because Agamemnon will not restore for ransom the daughter of one of his priests whom the Greek leader had taken as his prize in the general allotment of spoils. Apollo has sent a plague to infest the Greek camp. In a council called by Achilles, Agamemnon reluctantly agrees to give up his prize but haughtily vows to make up his loss by depriving Achilles of his slave girl Briseis, also a spoil of war. Thus slighted and dishonoured, Achilles angrily withdraws from the fighting. In Achilles' eyes Agamemnon abuses the power he has as leader of the Greeks and is guilty of *hybris*, arrogant behaviour that offends the gods (I, 203). After the quarrel, Achilles asks his goddess mother to persuade Zeus to grant the Trojans success so that the Greeks will be forced to recognise his worth. Zeus agrees and the Trojans advance from the city to the camp upon the plain. Faced with this threat, the Greeks petition Achilles to return; Agamemnon, who privately admits his error, offers gifts of compensation going beyond what was required by good form alone. But the insult to his honour is so deeply felt that Achilles remains obdurate.

To the other Greeks it seems that Achilles is arrogantly acting as if he were a law unto himself. His response may seem disproportionate but it has its origin in something exceptionally pure and noble. No other Homeric hero has the aspiration for glory in so intense a form, for Achilles is not fighting for revenge or the defence of loved ones, neither has any other Homeric hero consciously made the sacrifice that is reflected in his stark choice. With this purity of motive, Achilles has an absolute sense of his own worth and of the honour due to him because of it. Any diminution of this honour diminishes the whole man and renders his choice of life null and void. There is honourable truth in such feeling and Achilles honours this single truth so absolutely that he is blind to all other truths, so that this purity of motive proves the ruin not only of many others but of himself too.

The Trojans have further success, and even his great comrade in arms Patroclus remarks that while doctors are treating the wounded Greek leaders, Achilles alone is untreatable (XVI, 21– 35). When Achilles relents to the point of allowing Patroclus to fight in his place wearing his armour, there are the first signs of a recognition of his error, as Achilles admits that a man cannot be angry for ever (XVI, 60–1). The concern for his honour is still overriding: Patroclus must only save the ships; he must not fight on to Troy or he will diminish the honour of Achilles (XVI, 80–90). But there is magnanimity as well as irony in his final wish that both he and Patroclus may survive to take Troy together (XVI, 97–100).

The calamitous death of Patroclus, whom he loves more than his own life (XVIII, 81–2), becomes the calamity of Achilles. When the news reaches him, Achilles in conversation with Thetis fully recognises his own error and folly. The gods have done much for him but there is no pleasure in achievement any more. He is ready for death, regrets his special destiny as the son of a goddess and recognises the insidious effects of anger that can darken the wisest mind, is sweeter than honey and spreads like smoke. But the quarrel must be put behind him, and he yields to necessity, accepting the fate which Thetis has revealed to him. He resolves to seek glory and the death of Hector (XVIII, 79–126).

In the ensuing fight, Achilles, whose purity of motive is now tainted by the desire for revenge into which his anger has been newly channelled, is resolute for death. His encounter with Aeneas (Book XX) has none of the chivalry that characterised the duels of Paris and Menelaus (Book III), Glaucus and Diomedes (Book VI), or Hector and Ajax (Book VII) in the earlier part of the poem. He captures twelve young Trojans to sacrifice on the pyre of Patroclus (XXI, 27–32, and XXIII, 175–6). He is deaf to the pleas of the suppliant Lycaon whom he had spared on a previous occasion (XXI, 34–135). His arrogant challenge to the river god (XXI, 136–383) contrasts with the restrained war against the gods waged by Diomedes with the support of Athene (Book V). The darkening moral tone of the poem is apparent in the many images of corpses exposed to dogs and carrion birds. In the final combat, the chivalrous Hector proposes a compact whereby the victor does no more than take the spoils of the loser, restoring his body for burial (XXII, 254–9). These are the conditions that had been agreed on in the earlier combat with Ajax (VII, 76–86). Achilles will have none of it: 'Men cannot make compacts with lions' (XXII, 261–72). After the fatal blow, Achilles in a murderous mood tells Hector that the dogs and birds of prey will pull him to pieces (XXII, 335–6). With his dying breath Hector again begs for mercy for his corpse (XXII, 338–43). Achilles again refuses in fury; he wishes he could tear him up into pieces and eat him himself, but certainly the dogs

and birds will feast upon him (**XXII**, 345–54). His cruel spirit is
well suggested in the version of George Chapman (1611).

'Dog', he replied, 'urge not my ruth by parents, soul nor
  knees.
I would to God that any rage would let me eat thee raw,
Sliced into pieces, so beyond the right of any law
I taste thy merits. And believe it flies the force of man
To rescue thy head from the dogs. Give all the gold they can,
If ten or twenty times so much as friends would rate thy
  price
Were tendered here, with vows of more, to buy the cruelties
I here have vowed, and, after that, thy father with his gold
Would free thy self – all that should fail to let thy mother
  hold
Solemnities of death with thee and do thee such a grace
To mourn thy whole corpse on a bed – which piecemeal I'll
  deface
With fowls and dogs.'

He then fastens Hector's body to his chariot and drags him away.
For several days at dawn he hauls Hector's corpse three times
around the funeral mound of Patroclus. As she had said farewell
to Hector, Andromache recalled how Achilles had chivalrously
reverenced the bodies of her family killed at Thebe (**VI**, 414–28).
How far below his previous magnanimity has he now fallen: so
far that his behaviour becomes offensive to the gods, who put a
stop to it (**XXIV**, 1–92).

In the final book comes the second and fullest recognition
scene in the meeting with Priam. Here Achilles is restored to
humanity by the pleas of Priam who reminds him of his own
aged father Peleus. In his gentle treatment of Priam there is true
magnanimity. Achilles looks beyond his own grief and anger, and
comes to a calm and steady recognition that men can do no
more than bear the indiscriminate mixture of good and bad that
comes from Zeus. In the examples of Peleus and Priam he sees
the insecurity and incompleteness of human happiness; grief is of
little use in the face of the inevitability of human suffering
(**XXIV**, 518–51). The pathos of this great speech is well conveyed in the version of Alexander Pope.

'Alas! what weight of anguish hast thou known?
Unhappy prince! thus guardless and alone
To pass through foes, and thus undaunted face
The man whose fury has destroyed thy race?
A strength proportioned to thy woes you feel.
Rise then: let reason mitigate our care:
To mourn, avails not: man is born to bear.
Such is, alas! the gods' severe decree;
They, only they, are blest, and only free.
Two urns by Jove's high throne have ever stood,
The source of evil one, and one of good;
From thence the cup of mortal man he fills,
Blessings to these, to those distributes ills;
To most, he mingles both: the wretch decreed
To taste the bad, unmixed, is cursed indeed;
Pursued by wrongs, by meagre famine driven,
He wanders, outcast both of earth and heaven.
The happiest taste not happiness sincere,
But find the cordial draught is dashed with care.
Who more than Peleus shone in wealth and power?
What stars concurring blest his natal hour?
A realm, a goddess, to his wishes given,
Graced by the gods with all the gifts of heaven!
One evil yet o'ertakes his latest day,
No race succeeding to imperial sway:
An only son! and he (alas!) ordained
To fall untimely in a foreign land!
See him, in Troy, the pious care decline
Of his weak age, to live the curse of thine!
Thou too, old man, hast happier days beheld;
In riches once, in children once excelled; . . .
But since the god his hand has pleased to turn,
And fill thy measure from his bitter urn,
What sees the sun, but hapless heroes' falls?
War, and the blood of men, surround thy walls!
What must be, must be. Bear thy lot, nor shed
These unavailing sorrows o'er the dead;
Thou canst not call him from the Stygian shore,
But thou alas! may'st live to suffer more!'

In his acceptance and resolution here we find the noble simplicity and quiet grandeur that have often been acknowledged to be the hallmarks of a classic spirit. How vulnerable and fragile this is before the onset of passion is wonderfully clear in the momentary anger that flares up in Achilles when Priam is impatient to see Hector. But Achilles collects himself, and he urges Priam to share a meal. The taking of food symbolises the practical acceptance of continuing life and the recognition that even the passion of grief must yield to necessity. Amid the ruins of human hope and in the knowledge of imminent death, Achilles for the first time sees life steadily and sees it whole.

In concentrating therefore upon the defeat of heroic expectation by folly and passion and in organising his poem around the anger in such a way that we see in the passionate nature of the hero the cause both of his greatness and also of his great error, Homer has made a tragedy out the heroic myth. Indeed the Greeks came to regard Homer as the father of tragedy and it is possible to see in the *Iliad* the elements later isolated by the fourth-century philosopher and critic Aristotle in his *Poetics*: error (*hamartia*) in Agamemnon's folly and Achilles' persistence, reversal (*peripeteia*) in the arming of Patroclus and the consequent calamity (*pathos*) in his death, and finally recognition (*anagnoresis*) in the conversation of Achilles first with Thetis and then with Priam.

Unity of design

In the *Iliad* we can also see the embodiment of all those tendencies to concentration and unity that are the hallmarks of Greek art. Here many cited the judgement of Aristotle in his *Poetics*:

A plot does not possess unity, as some people suppose, merely because it is about one man. Many things, countless thing indeed, may happen to one man, and some of them will not contribute to any kind of unity; and similarly he may carry out many actions from which no single unified action will emerge. . . . Homer, exceptional in this as in all other respects, seems, whether by art or by instinct, to have been well aware of what was required. . . . although the Trojan War had a beginning and an end, he did not attempt to put

13

the whole of it into the poem; it would have been too large a subject to be taken in all at once, and if he had limited its length, the diversity of incident would have made it too complicated. As it is, he has selected one part of the story and has introduced many incidents from other parts as episodes, such as the Catalogue of Ships and other episodes with which he gives variety to his poem.

(VIII, XXIII)

In concentrating the main action of the *Iliad* upon the anger of Achilles Homer does not waste time in telling us about unessential aspects of Achilles' life and character that do not have a bearing upon his anger, nor does he obscure his main theme by telling the tale of Troy from the beginning. He begins in the middle of things in the ninth year of the siege of Troy selecting only those particulars that relate to his central theme, which has a clear beginning in the quarrel scene, a middle in all the consequences that flow from it and an end in the resolution of the anger. The clear chain of cause and effect in the main action has all the requirements of the classically well-made plot that Aristotle made famous in the *Poetics*. Of course this plot is diversified, extended and enriched by many episodes, but they do not take us to places far away from the plain of Troy or extend the temporal framework within which the main action takes place. In the final analysis they are subordinate to the main action of the irreducible plot.

Within his concentrated action, which takes place within a period of a few days, Homer has nevertheless skilfully interwoven the whole Trojan story. When the scene changes from the Greek camp to the Trojan city in Book Three, the action involving Paris, Helen and Menelaus and the presence of Aphrodite the goddess of love puts before us the protagonists of the original quarrel and indirectly recounts the causes of the war. The second scene in Troy in Book Six where Hector says farewell to Andromache and to his son Astyanax is full of foreboding and looks ominously to the future. The future doom of Troy features predominantly in further forebodings and prophecies and in the pronouncements of the gods, so that the main action is seen to be part of a much larger design involving the whole Trojan War.

From the concentration and unity of a clear and simple design

14

stems the universality for which Greek art has always been famous. For the main plot of the *Iliad* gives us a pattern of behaviour that in its causes and effects represents a probable if not inevitable sequence. Underneath all that is particular and individual, the anger is typical in its causes and consequences, and it is Homer's method or art that enables us to see this. Homer the artist has therefore accomplished in his poetry all that Aristotle the philosopher and critic held to be the end of art; he has imposed form and order on the undifferentiated matter and random chaos of life, thus enabling us to see through the particular to the universal. This imposition of form is not therefore simply an aesthetic matter. It is the means whereby the poet clarifies and communicates moral truth about the human world he is representing in his poem.

THE *ODYSSEY*

Aristotle remarks that while the *Iliad* has a simple plot that involves emotion and calamity, the *Odyssey* is complex and revolves upon character (*Poetics*, **XXIV**). It is on the character of Odysseus that the action principally turns. The essence of his characterisation is simple and clear, and is indicated in the various epithets given to him. In the opening line of the poem he is said to be *polytropos*, variously translated as the man of many ways, many turns or many parts. He is also *polymetis* and *polymechanos*, the man of much contrivance and many devices, and of course *polytlas*, much-suffering and much-enduring. He is a man of great versatility and great virtuosity who has seen cities and known the minds of men; he survives by reliance upon his wits and by virtue of his intelligence. Though Odysseus is famous for his 'Odyssey', his long journey to strange lands and distant places, Homer starts his *Odyssey* at a point when his hero is near the end of his journey, after he has been a prisoner of the nymph Calypso on the island of Ogygia for seven years. The main part of his 'Odyssey' is narrated in the form of an after-dinner speech to the Phaeacians, on whose island he is shipwrecked after he has left Calypso. The remainder of the poem, its second half, is entirely concerned with the situation in Ithaca and with Odysseus's successful efforts to regain mastery of his own household.

The poem starts with a dramatic representation of the

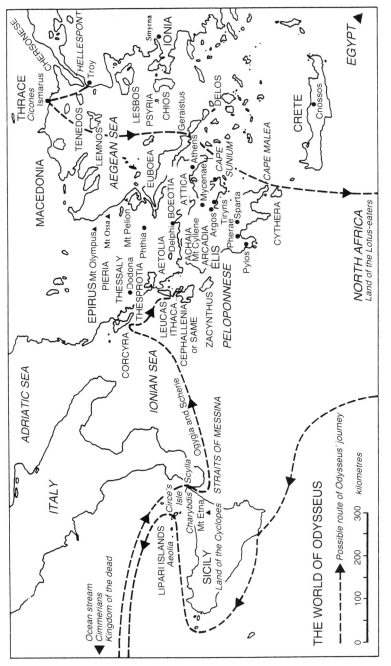

Figure 4   The world of Odysseus

disorder in Ithaca in Odysseus' absence. Nine years after the Trojan War, the sons of the neighbouring aristocracy are competing for the hand of his wife Penelope in marriage, and riotously consuming his substance in feasting and nightly entertainment. The choice lies with Penelope, and the wooers are pressing their suit till she chooses one of their number. In an Ithacan assembly, Odysseus' only son Telemachus, who has just recently come of age, attempts to eject the suitors, who are in no mood to go. The people in Ithaca are entirely passive, there being no external authority to which appeal can be made in Homeric society. Telemachus determines to journey to Pylos, the home of Nestor, and to Sparta, the home of Menelaus, in order to seek news of his father to end the uncertainty. The position of Penelope is delicate. She wishes to remain loyal to Odysseus and does not want to choose a successor, but the assertion of Telemachus, which exposes him to danger (the suitors have a plot to ambush him on his return which he is only able to evade by use of his wits), puts new pressure upon her. The situation in Ithaca is most unstable; events are taking an ugly turn and entering a dangerous and critical stage. The judgement on the suitors at the beginning of the poem and throughout is clear. Their riotous actions and insulting speeches are a gross breach of Homeric manners. The line between unseemly behaviour and downright wickedness is clearly crossed in the plot to ambush and kill Telemachus. The moral outline of the poem is simple and clear; the stage is set at the opening for the ultimate triumph of right over wrong in the poetic justice that is to be meted out in the reversal of fortune at the poem's climax.

The scene now shifts to Calypso's isle, where Odysseus is to be found in nostalgic mood, away from the goddess, yearning for his return home. The gods send their messenger Hermes to instruct Calypso to release the hero. Odysseus builds a raft, sets sail but is almost drowned when Poseidon, god of the seas, whose anger he incurred when he killed his son Polyphemus the Cyclops, raises a storm which blows him off course and shipwrecks him on Scherie, the island home of the Phaeacians.

This is an idealised and romantic setting, well suited to serve as the backdrop for Odysseus's account of his fabulous adventures. It is in fact his last port of call in the world of romance before he returns to the realities of Ithaca. Here he is courteously received by the Phaeacians, to whom he tells the story of his past wanderings from Troy.

Declaring his identity at the opening of his retrospective narrative, he announces that he is famous among men for all manner of stratagems (IX, 19). The word he uses here is *dolos*, denoting wiles, craft, stratagems or cunning. The account of his adventures reveals him to be the wily and versatile Greek who has been tested in a wide variety of experiences. In contrast to his companions, who against his warnings foolishly kill the oxen of Hyperion the sun god, his thirst for adventure is tempered by the restraining influence of good sense. The tales also enhance his character and status before he embarks upon his final encounter with the suitors.

The Phaeacians honour him with gifts in admiration for his physical and mental prowess and convey him to Ithaca in one of their magic ships. He is left alone sleeping upon the shore. On awakening he fails to recognise his native home. When Athene appears disguised as a shepherd, he invents the first of several Cretan tales to keep his identity secret, in which he says he is on the run after a homicide, a realistic tale very different in character from the folk tales involving the Cyclops and Circe which we have previously heard. In the stratagem of the tale, revealing Odysseus' habitual inventiveness, caution and craft, the hero shows himself worthy of the attention of the goddess, who is amused by it, feeling a natural affinity with one who is *epetes*, variously rendered as 'of soft or fluent speech', 'sociable' or 'civilised', *angkinoos*, of quick understanding and *echephron*, self-possessed, controlled, prudent (XIII, 332). These are the qualities of mind and intelligence by virtue of which Odysseus is favoured by the goddess and succeeds in the supreme stratagem whereby he regains the mastery of his own house.

Athene initiates the plan by which Odysseus, disguised as a beggar, will find out for himself what is happening in Ithaca and take advantage of any opportunity that comes his way. To this end he uses the disguise to test loyalties and only reveals himself to those whose aid is necessary. He first visits the hut of his faithful steward Eumaeus, who offers him generous hospitality. Their encounter is full of poignant ironies, not least when Eumaeus believes the Cretan tale told by the stranger but not his oath that Odysseus is shortly to return. Here he encounters Telemachus who on his return from Sparta has just evaded the ambush laid for him by the suitors. Then comes the first of several recognition scenes in which Odysseus reveals himself to his son. Together they plot the suitors' downfall and set off for the palace.

In the insulting behaviour of the suitors Odysseus experiences their iniquities at first hand and sees the sufferings endured by his household, in particular those of his loyal wife Penelope, who welcomes him generously without knowing who he is and questions him about Odysseus. Their long conversation (which is interrupted by the recognition scene involving his old nurse Eurycleia), since it is centred upon the absent husband actually present, is full of irony and pathos. Penelope unburdens herself to the stranger, telling him of the pressures she reluctantly faces to remarry. Odysseus silently grieves for his sorrowing wife, trying to comfort her with a tale that he has recently seen Odysseus whom he predicts will soon return. Penelope, however, does not believe him and, in the course of their conversation, she comes to the momentous decision to arrange for the contest with the great bow of Odysseus; she will marry the man who can string it. This is the opportunity that Odysseus has been waiting for. When none of the suitors proves adequate to the task, he asks for the chance to try himself. Telemachus ensures that he is given the bow and so starts the killing of the suitors.

The scene is now set for the climactic recognition scene between husband and wife. Penelope is cautious and in turn tests Odysseus. When she finally suspends her disbelief she compares her position to that of Helen (who had yielded to the stranger Paris, who then abducted her to Troy causing the war with the Greeks), thus crystallising for the audience the prudence of her conduct by contrast. In the final book the scene shifts to the underworld where the shades of the suitors tell their version of their miserable end to the shades of Achilles and Agamemnon, who sets the seal of heroic approval upon the action of Odysseus and extols the virtue of Penelope. 'Blessed is Odysseus in the great virtue of his wife, always loyal to him. The fame of her virtue (*arete*) will never perish, and the immortals will fashion a beautiful song in honour of Penelope the wise' (XXIV, 192–202: *echephron*, having understanding, prudent or self-possessed, the epithet given earlier by Athene to Odysseus). Agamemnon, who had been murdered by his own wife Clytemnestra and her paramour Aegisthus on his return from Troy, speaks feelingly here. So many Greek myths show the dominance of cruel and treacherous passions indulged without any restraint of civilised feeling or morality, but in the happy ending of the *Odyssey*, Homer rewards the wise restraint of his characters and serenely celebrates the most basic natural bonds of human life between parent and child and above all between husband and wife.

Homer endows Odysseus with that quality of restraint that he exhibits himself in the controlling artistry of his poems, manifested both in their measured style and their balanced structure. Both poems may be said to recommend in different ways the two great maxims of Greek culture inscribed on the temple of Apollo at Delphi: *gnothi seauton*, Know Thyself, and *meden agan*, Nothing in Excess.

HOMERIC IDEALS: CIVILISED SOCIAL LIVING

The end of the *Odyssey* restores the conditions in which civilised living is again possible. An idealised version of Homeric civilisation is the tranquil world that Odysseus enters when he arrives in Scherie, a rich land whose seafaring inhabitants know of war only as a subject of song while pursuing the occupations of peace. They are indirectly contrasted with their old neighbours the Cyclopes (VI, 5), who dwell in caves, do not practise agriculture and are said to be *athemistes*, that is, having no respect for *themis* (custom, law or equity), but who live each a law unto himself in the primitive state of nature where the individual will is not controlled and civilised by the social bond. While the response of the Cyclops to a visiting stranger is that of the savage, the benevolent Phaeacians show respect for the suppliant, unconditionally welcoming Odysseus without knowing who he is. In their generous treatment of their visitor, whom they honour with gifts, and in the delicate manners exhibited in the royal household between king, queen and princess, we see the highest standards of Homeric civilisation. Odysseus reciprocates, himself showing exquisite manners in his delicate and considerate dealings with the young Nausicaa.

These standards are reflected too in the treatment given to Telemachus as a guest at Pylos and Sparta, in the simple piety of Nestor and his relationship with his sons, and in the humanity of

Menelaus and his tranquil relationship with Helen, now for-
given. But the most striking example of moral excellence in
the poem is the compassion shown to Odysseus in disguise as
an apparently destitute beggar by Eumaeus, Telemachus and
Penelope. These are the civilised standards by which we are to
judge the shameless behaviour of the suitors, who lack *aidos*,
that quality of restraint that enforces respect for the laws of
hospitality and decency in human relations.

In other respects Scherie represents a world redolent of Greek
ideals. The striking description of its beautiful garden and
magnificent palace (a reminder of the sophisticated monuments
of Mycenaean culture) evokes a world of order, harmony and
proportion, a cultivated place of material splendour in which the
physical and the artistic are equally valued. In this setting
Homer endows his hero as he sets out for the palace with a
beauty that has come to be regarded as the Greek ideal:

> Athene made him seem taller and sturdier than ever and
> caused the bushy locks to hang from his head thick as the
> petals of the hyacinth in bloom. Just as a craftsman trained
> by Hephaestus and herself in the secrets of his art takes pains
> to put a graceful finish to his work by overlaying silver-ware
> with gold, she finished now by endowing his head and
> shoulders with added beauty. When Odysseus retired to sit
> down by himself on the sea-shore, he was radiant with
> comeliness and grace.
>
> (VI, 229–35)

Once there, he is entertained with food, drink, dancing and with
the songs of the minstrel. He is then invited to compete in the
Phaeacian games by one of the king's sons: 'you must surely be
an athlete, for nothing makes a man so famous for life as what he
can do with his hands and his feet' (VI, 146–8). He declines, but
another Phaeacian assails him with the taunt that he is a mere
trader concerned with profit. In less ideal circumstances we see
Odysseus deeply concerned with material things. Part of his
completeness as a human being is that he is not completely
ideal. But here his heroic spirit responds angrily to the Phaeacian rebuke with the remark that 'we cannot all hope to combine
the pleasing qualities of good looks, brains and eloquence' (VIII,
168). He then participates and excels, proving himself here the
all-round man comprising the Greek ideal.

HOMERIC IDEALS: POETRY AND ART

As he begins the narrative of his tales, Odysseus gives voice to a further Homeric ideal in his praise of the feast and the song:

> 'Lord Alcinous, it is indeed a lovely thing to hear a bard such as yours, with a voice like the gods'. I myself feel that there is nothing more delightful than when the festive mood reigns in a whole people's hearts and the banqueters listen to a minstrel from their seats in the hall, while the tables before them are laden with bread and meat, and a steward carries round the wine he has drawn from the bowl and fills their cups. This, to my way of thinking, is something like perfection.'
>
> (IX, 1–11)

Whatever partiality Homer had to his own profession, there can be no doubt that the bard was held in especial honour in Homeric culture. In the ideal society of the Phaeacians, the blind bard Demodocus, whose name means 'honoured by the people', has a special place. In Ithaca Homer makes it clear that Phemius, whose name means 'praiser', sings at the banquet of the suitors 'by necessity' (I, 154). The motif is repeated in the suitor – slaying when Phemius, here called Terpiades ('the son of delight'), throws himself at the mercy of Odysseus:

> 'You will repent it later if you kill a minstrel like me, who sings for gods and men. I had no teacher but myself. All kinds of song spring unpremeditated to my lips; and I feel that I could sing for you as I could sing for a god.'
>
> (XXII, 344–9)

Phemius is spared, but the direct appeal of the priest Leodes to Odysseus goes unheeded and he is cut down with the rest.

In Homeric society the roles of poet and priest, so often confused in earlier societies, are thoroughly distinct. It is worth noting too that while Homeric man is not irreligious, most of the practices such as sacrifices and funerals that are presided over by priests in other societies are conducted by the heroes themselves. The custodian confirming the identity, commemorating the values and transmitting the ideals of Homeric culture from generation to generation is not, as in Egyptian society, the priest, but is the bard like Phemius and Demodocus who sang, as Achilles sings in his tent at *Iliad* X, 189, of the *klea andron* ('the great deeds of famous men'). The old tag that Homer was the Bible of the Greeks serves to remind us that while the Homeric poems were indeed accorded the special status in Greek culture and education that the Bible has often had in the Judeao-Christian world, the Hellenic spirit is as different from the Hebraic recorded in the Bible as it is from the Egyptian, whose conservative priestly caste has left no great texts. Unlike the prophets of the Old Testament, Homer is the reverse of other-worldly; he celebrates the vibrancy of the human spirit in the here and now, manifested in the godlike actions of his heroes.

The Homeric bard, of course, is not merely the conduit through which culture is transmitted, for he himself, like Demo-docus and Phemius who are 'inspired by the god', is the creative agent who transmutes the raw material of the world around him into art. The fullest and most dynamic portrait of the artist in Homer is of the artist as god himself when we see the divine artificer Hephaestus in the *Iliad* forging the shield of Achilles and recreating on it the whole Homeric world, beginning with the sun, the moon and the constellations, and ending with the Ocean stream, which just as it encircles the world in Homer, encircles the rim of the divine artefact.

Homer gives us a vivid impression of the shield's manufacture, as the god vigorously sets about his task. The divine craftsman-ship of the plastic artist finds its counterpart in the poetic energy with which Homer invests his descriptions of the scenes on the shield. In these, there is so much activity and movement that rationalistic critics have been offended because the descriptions no longer accurately represent what is a static object. But Homer is not interested in accurate representation, in verisimilitude, but in lively representation. The art of Homer is not to give us finished pictures but pictures in the making. Homeric art is not still, like a Grecian urn, but always moving and full of energy.

The god first creates two beautiful cities. The first is a city at peace in which weddings are celebrated with music, singing, feasting and dancing. In the market assembly of the people two litigants disputing claims of compensation for a homicide put their case before a tribunal of elders who give judgement and expound the law. In contrast to this picture of peaceful activity and the rule of law is the second city, which is in a state of siege. There is an ambush and a bloody battle. Five agricultural scenes follow: the ploughing of a field with a drink of mellow wine for the ploughman; the harvest on the king's estate with a feast for the labourers; the grape-picking by young men and women to the accompaniment of music, song and dancing; the herding of cattle with the intrusion of a lion who carries off a bellowing bull; and lastly the grazing ground for sheep. The final picture is of young men and women dancing to music and delighting a crowd of onlookers.

Though many of the scenes are idyllic, the overall representation is not idealised in the sense that men are represented as better than they are. Even in the first city at peace, a homicide has been committed. In the second city, the soldiers engage in battle, fight and drag off their dead like real living men (*Iliad* XVII, 539). It is apparent that what the poet admires most is the realism of the picture and the ability of the god to bring it all to life. The city at war has a representational beauty, justifying Homer's description of both cities as beautiful (XVII, 491).

There are several touches that testify to the craftsmanship of the god. In the city at war the gods are larger than life and wrought in gold. In the picture of the ploughing the unploughed field is made of gold; behind the plough the colour of the soil is black as in real life, a marvel to behold (XVIII, 549). The vineyard is gold, the grapes are black, the ditches are blue and the fences tin. The cows are of gold and tin. The poet appreciates the divine craftsmanship whereby the god makes the most of his various materials to ensure that vital details stand out in relief.

The culmination of the celebration of the artist comes in the final picture on the shield (XVIII, 590–606), the dancing on a beautiful dance floor likened to the famous one built at Cnossos by Daedalus, the legendary Cretan artist and craftsman. Hephaestus began the shield with a joyful celebration of weddings with music, singing and dancing. He ends with a picture that celebrates youth and movement in the delight of the dance. The movement of the dancers is compared to the wheel of a potter. The immediate point of comparison is speed but the figure also suggests the perfect symmetry of the circle that results in a finished work of art. A great crowd gathers, delighting in the spectacle of the dance, and the bard sings to the accompaniment of the lyre. In the midst of the dancers acrobats perform in time to the music. In the whole scene the dominant impression is one of joyous celebration of physical energy. But the dance is organised energy so that the picture also celebrates the power of art apparent in the underlying pattern of the dance, the mention of Daedalus, the image of the potter's wheel, and the presence of the bard and his music. Though it does not obtrude (they are not dancing a minuet) there is a formality and order underlying the energy and spontaneity of the dance, so that this final picture on the shield is a fitting climax encapsulating the essence of Homeric art.

THE GREEK LOVE OF BEAUTY AND HOMER'S STYLE

For the modern world the Hellenic spirit has come to be particularly associated with Athens, and if the word Athenian is synonymous with the cultured and cultivated, it is because the Athenians yielded to the spirit of Homer more completely than other Greeks, like the Spartans, who turned their backs upon it. 'For we are lovers of beauty without extravagance and lovers of wisdom without unmanliness.' These famous words, put into the mouth of the Athenian leader Pericles by the historian Thucydides (II, 40), have been regarded as defining the Athenian spirit in its highest manifestation. The Greek love of beauty is memorably expressed in the reactions of the old men of Troy as they catch sight of Helen coming to the tower: 'Who on earth,' they asked one another, 'could blame the Trojans and Achaean men-at-arms for suffering so long for such a woman's sake? Indeed she is the very image of an immortal goddess' (*Iliad* III, 156–8). After they have eaten, Priam expresses his wonder at the stature and beauty of Achilles, who is the very image of a god (*Iliad* XXIV, 629–33). The perfect beauty of the anthropomorphic gods is constantly implied in the use of recurring epithets like 'golden Aphrodite'. The value set upon beauty is apparent in the fate of the godlike Ganymede, a mortal who grew to be the most beautiful youth in the world and because of his good looks was stolen by the gods to be the cup bearer of Zeus (XX, 232–5). The famous fifth-century sculptor Pheidias is said to have been inspired by Homer's majestic description of the dark eyebrows and ambrosial locks of Zeus (*Iliad* I, 528–9) when he made his famous statue of Zeus at Olympia. The description of the messenger of the gods, Hermes, with his golden sandals and wand, 'looking like a princely youth at the most graceful time when the beard first begins to grow' (*Iliad* XXIV, 339–48), fits exactly his representation in the statues of later time.

Homer celebrates the beauty of the persons, places and material objects that he describes in his poems, but a poet's feeling for beauty is chiefly reflected in his own use of language and style. And here the first remarks must be reserved for the graceful beauty of Homer's verse and its almost magical metrical harmony. One of his Greek admirers writing in the last decades of the first century, Dionysius of Halicarnassus, cites (in the third chapter of his treatise *On Literary Composition*), the opening lines of Book Sixteen of the *Odyssey*, which describes the scene in Eumaeus' hut and the reaction of his dogs at the moment when Telemachus returns, as an instance of Homer's ability to make enchanting poetry out of the simplest and most common-place incidents of everyday life. Dionysius points out that all the words that Homer uses here are quite ordinary, such as might be used by a farmer, a sailor or anyone who is not concerned with elegant speech. Neither is the language in the least figurative. When the lines are broken up, the language is utterly undistinguished.

> When Telemachus arrived, Odysseus and the worthy swine-herd were preparing their breakfast in the hut by the light of dawn, after stirring up the fire and sending the herdsmen off with the pigs to the pastures. The dogs, usually so obstreperous, not only did not bark at the newcomer but greeted him with wagging tails. Odysseus heard footsteps and at the same moment observed the dogs' friendly behaviour. Immediately alert, he turned to his companion and said: 'Eumaeus, you have a visitor: I can hear his steps. He must be a friend of yours or someone familiar here, for the dogs are wagging their tails instead of barking.'

The prose version bears out what Dionysius has to say. The beauty of the poetry derives from the metrical order of its composition. Unfortunately, it is not possible to find any verse translation that is able to convey the poetic effect of Homer's Greek in passages of plain and simple description such as this. However, Homer's stylistic range is as varied as his subject matter, and translators have been inspired to poetic heights in passages of pathos and grandeur.

26

In his treatise *On the Sublime*, probably written in the first century AD and usually attributed to the Greek rhetorician Longinus, the author cites many passages from Homer, often in connection with the gods, to illustrate Homeric grandeur, for he regards Homer as a poet who works pre-eminently in the grand manner. By sublimity 'Longinus' does not merely mean grandeur. He defines the true sublime as any literary passage that has the power to elevate the reader and take him out of himself. The truly beautiful and sublime is what can be seen to have this effect on diverse people in different times (*On the Sublime*, VII). One such passage that has been much admired is the moment when Hector takes his farewell of Andromache in Book Six of the *Iliad*. There is the grandeur of Hector's prayer for a heroic future for his child, which is full of pathos and irony because of Hector's foreboding and the reader's knowledge that Troy will fall (when the child is cruelly thrown off the battlements). This is admirably rendered in the heroic couplet by the seventeenth-century translator, John Dryden.

> 'Parent of Gods and men, propitious Jove,
> And you bright synod of the powers above;
> On this my son your gracious powers bestow;
> Grant him to live, and great in arms to grow;
> To reign in Troy, to govern with renown,
> To shield the people, and assert the crown:
> That, when hereafter he from war shall come,
> And bring his Trojans peace and triumph home,
> Some aged man, who lives this act to see,
> And who in former times remembered me,
> May say the son in fortitude and fame
> Outgoes the mark, and drowns his father's name:
> That at these words his mother may rejoice,
> And add her suffrage to the public voice.'

But in this scene of great pathos and grandeur is the human reality of the small child's fear of the nodding plume of Hector's helmet, which causes laughter amidst the tears and makes the moment of parting one of tender intimacy, so that heroism is given a fully human context. This simple and direct portrayal of human nature is unhampered by any distracting notion of false grandeur either in human behaviour or in artistic expression. Homer's comprehensiveness can include the familiar touch, can descend to particular details of common human experience and can tolerate the intrusion of the comic. Discussion of these passages may serve to suggest that Homer's style has an unaffected beauty that is entirely without rhetorical extravagance or ornamental excess, and that the beauty of it springs from the delicate sense of decorum and propriety with which the artist's language is in perfect harmony with what he seeks to express.

Beauty without ornamental excess and a perfect harmony of content and form wherein the artist's expression is controlled by a restraining vision of what is truly natural – these are the hallmarks of classic art, miraculously perfect like the goddess of beauty herself at the moment of birth, in the poetic genius of archaic Greece.

2

HISTORY

The final association, formed of several villages, is the city or state (*polis*). For all practical purposes the process is now complete; self-sufficiency has been reached and so, while it started as a means of securing life itself, it is now in a position to secure the good life.

Aristotle, *Politics*, 1252

THE CITY STATE BEFORE THE PERSIAN WARS

The most striking feature of the political organisation of the Greek world in the archaic and classical eras was its division into countless small autonomous city states, which, despite constant warring and inter-state rivalry and in spite of various attempts by the more powerful states to establish hegemony, never combined into anything approaching what we think of today as a nation state, until unification was forced upon them by foreign conquest in the late fourth century. When Plato in the 380s designed his ideal state in the *Republic* and when Aristotle considered more practical alternatives in his *Politics* of the 330s, it was their common assumption that the natural unit of political life was the *polis*, a city state like Athens or Sparta. (The population of Periclean Athens is estimated to have been about 300,000, of whom about 170,000 were citizens, 30,000 were aliens and 100,000 were slaves.)

With the exception of the Homeric poems, nearly all the great creative achievements of Greek civilisation recorded in this volume in the fields of literature, philosophy, science and art came into being in the heyday of the city state in the fifth and fourth centuries. The ascendancy of Macedon, itself not a city state but a scattered tribal federation ruled by an autocratic monarchy, evident after the battle of Chaeronea in 338 and confirmed after the battle of Crannon in 322, traditionally marks the end of the classical era and the beginning of a new, less creative, phase of Greek civilisation usually called the Hellenistic age. The development and workings of the city state which provided the framework for the advanced civilisation of the Greeks are therefore a primary consideration, and since many of the achievements of the Greek world are the legacy of one state about which we know more than any other and since that state gave the world its first experience of democracy, the present chapter, which is designed to offer a brief historical outline of the Greek world, will concentrate upon Athens.

Athens is mentioned in the Homeric poems (the Athenian contingent comprises fifty ships) but the city is not the home of any of the great heroes, as Sparta is the home of Menelaus. And the Mycenaean world to which the Homeric poems look back is one in which the basic unit consisting of the royal household and outlying farms, like that of Odysseus in Ithaca, is smaller than the developed city state. Despite the boisterous contribution of the common man, Thersites, at the council of the Greeks at Troy in the *Iliad* (II, 209–77), and despite the existence of an assembly of the people to which Telemachus makes his appeal in the *Odyssey* (II, 7), the political and social organisation of the Greek world as represented in the Homeric poems is thoroughly aristocratic. In war, all the fighting is conducted by the great nobles themselves. In peace, power lies with the lord of the palace and, in his absence, there is no external authority to which appeal can be made. The people of Ithaca are entirely passive. Nevertheless, in the description of the city at peace on the great shield of Achilles, we clearly see the beginnings of public justice and criminal law; in the market place, the *agora*, two men in dispute over a homicide argue their case before the city elders. Though Homer uses the word *polis* for city, the word does not yet describe the developed city state which existed in the classical period. Yet paradoxically, at the time when the Homeric poems are now generally considered to have been composed, in the eighth century after the Bronze Age Mycenaean culture had long been subdued by the Dorians coming from the north in about 1120, the city state was well established.

In the case of Athens, the first stage in the evolution of the developed state was the unification of Attica, whereby Athens subdued other settlements in Attica with the result that all the inhabitants of Attica, a region of about a thousand square miles, whether or not they lived in the city, became Athenians. Long before written records, this unification was associated with the mythical hero Theseus. Thereafter the successors of Theseus were supposed to have ruled as kings, but by the seventh century the leadership of the city was in the hands of nine officials called archons (rulers) who held office annually and then automatically became members of the council which met on the hill of Ares, known as the Areopagus. Kingship has therefore become aristocracy and the history of the Athenian constitution thereafter is the slow extension of power beyond the confines of aristocratic families, the *eupatridai*, or the well-born, to the wealthy and then more generally to the lower orders.

In the late seventh and sixth centuries the rule of the *eupatridai* at Athens and of aristocracies in Greece generally was challenged by individuals aiming at tyranny by exploiting the discontent of those excluded from power. One such attempt, and one of the first recorded events at Athens, was by a former Olympic victor called Cylon, perhaps in the 630s. The severe code of the lawgiver Draco (whence Draconian), traditionally dated to 621–620, may have been an aristocratic response to popular discontent. At this time laws were for the first time formally written down. But when, like Aristotle, the Athenians looked back to their own constitutional development, the first great name with which they associated significant reform was that of Solon, who, Aristotle tells us, was appointed with special powers as mediator between the masses and the notables in his archonship of 594.

The problem he had to alleviate was first of all an economic one. The *eupatridai* had reduced many of the poorer citizens who had offered their persons as security for loans to the condition of serfdom and actual slavery. This practice, as well as cancelling all existing debts, Solon henceforth forbade in his *seisachtheia* or shaking off of burdens. He prohibited the export of agricultural produce, except oil, to encourage more equitable distribution of food in the city. But he also changed the constitution, defining four classes according to the annual production of corn, oil and wine, and opened the archonship, and therefore the Areopagus, to the two highest classes. The third class could hold minor offices and was eligible for membership of the new *boule*, or council of 500, which must have taken over functions which had previously been the exclusive preserve of the old aristocratic council, though he confirmed the Areopagus in its ancient right of superintending the laws and acting as general guardian of the constitution. Nevertheless, even though Solon had not redistributed land, power had been extended beyond the well-born to include the wealthy so that aristocracy was becoming a broader-based oligarchy. But Aristotle finds the greatest reform to rest in the power he gave to all citizen classes, including the lowest, to hear appeals against magistrates' verdicts or to impose penalties in the assembly: 'This, they say, was the key to the future strength of the masses; for when the people control the ballot box, they are likewise masters of the constitution' (*The Athenian Constitution*, 9A).

However, discontent at Athens was rife, not only between classes but also between regions, to an extent that there developed three distinct groupings, centred upon the hill, the coast and the plain. The leader of the hill party of least privileged citizens, Peisistratus, managed to establish himself as tyrant, sole ruler, of Athens in 561. He was driven out, but with the help of mercenaries re-established himself and ruled from 546 until his death in 527. He made peace with the leading families and retained the forms of Solon's constitution ensuring that his own supporters held office. His rule was a period of economic success and cultural expansion. A native Attic coinage, making possible a new economic freedom, may be dated to about this time. In foreign policy, he consolidated Athenian interests in settlements around the Hellespont designed to promote trade and ensure the supply of Pontic corn. He had been involved in the worsting of Athens' neighbour and commercial rival, Megara, but otherwise did not involve Athens in foreign wars. In his time, black-figure Attic pottery was exported throughout the Mediterranean. He renewed the Great Panathenaic festival, where it is reported rhapsodes recited the Homeric poems. The Athenians did not look back to his rule as to a reign of cruelty; the word tyrant, meaning single ruler (Oedipus is called a 'tyrant' of Thebes), did not necessarily have the pejorative over tones it has acquired since. He was succeeded by his son Hippias, who was finally expelled from Athens in 510 by exiled

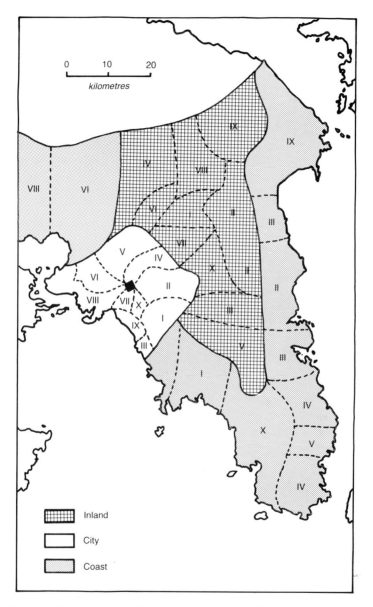

Figure 5 The reforms of Cleisthenes. Attica is split into three regions: the city, the inland and the coast. Each region has ten *trittyes*. Each tribe (represented by Roman numerals on the map) has one *trittys* from each region

aristocrats with the help of the Spartan king Cleomenes. The expulsion of the tyrants came to be regarded as a landmark in the evolution of the constitution.

In the struggle for power that followed, the leader of one of the aristocratic factions, Cleisthenes, who, according to the historian Herodotus, 'was getting the worst of it, managed to win popular support' (V, 66). He initiated democratic reforms by the reorganisation of existing institutions. All Greek states were divided into tribes based originally on ties of kin. At Athens there were four tribes with their own priests and leaders; as well as endowing their members with a sense of identity, they also served as subdivisions of the state for administrative and military purposes. They were dominated by the old aristocratic families. As membership was hereditary, those enfranchised by Solon and the tyrants were not enrolled in any tribe. Cleisthenes created ten new tribes made up of three subdivisions called *trittys*, each from quite different parts of the state. Each *trittys* was further subdivided into demes, membership of which was extended to all free citizens. Each deme, of which there were about 150, kept a record of its members and was represented on the *boule* (council) according to its size. The reorganisation, although seemingly highly artificial, was successful in extending the franchise, in breaking the local power of the *eupatridai* and in discouraging the kind of regional grouping that had been exploited by Peisistratus.

The institution of ostracism, so named from the potsherd or *ostrakon* on which a name was inscribed, is sometimes associated with Cleisthenes, though it was not used until 487. It may have been introduced as a safeguard against tyranny. If an ostracism was voted for by the assembly (*ekklesia*), it was subsequently held in the Agora under the supervision of the archons. A vote of 6,000 was required. The penalty entailed exile for ten years without confiscation of property.

By the beginning of the fifth century, therefore, although the main offices were still largely the preserve of the wealthy and the aristocratic, the ordinary citizens had, in theory, equality before the law, *isonomia*, and some measure of participation in the political process. Later Athenians recognised in their constitution after Cleisthenes the substantial beginnings of their radical democracy. Other Greek states developed on similar lines from aristocracy through tyranny to oligarchy, but oligarchy remained the predominant constitution; few states gave to the people the power invested in them at Athens in the assembly, the law court and the ballot box.

Nevertheless, at this time Athens was not the leading Greek city state; this position was undoubtedly occupied by Sparta, whose constitution had developed on its own distinct lines and for very different ends. Sparta was unique in retaining kingship, in fact a dual kingship, possibly a result of a coalition of two distinct tribal communities, each with its own king. They were the supreme commanders of the army, but in other respects their powers were circumscribed by three other institutions, the ephorate, the *gerousia* and the assembly. The ephors, five in number, were elected annually and were supposedly representatives of the people who had the power to bring the kings to account. Other judicial functions were divided between them and the *gerousia*, a council of twenty-eight aristocrats over 60 years of age in addition to the two kings. The council prepared matters to be brought before the assembly of all citizens over 30, the Spartiates, who did not have the power of discussion but whose assent by acclamation was necessary for the validity of any decree. However, the magistrate who presided over the proceedings of the assembly had the power of dissolving and annulling its decrees if they did not meet with approval. This very mixed constitution of checks and balances, which the Greeks believed had been laid down by the lawgiver Lycurgus, was thought to have developed as early as the seventh century and it remained unchanged throughout Sparta's history.

Sparta's supremacy owed much to the distinct state-training, the *agoge*, given to children of the Spartiates from the age of 7. After they had reached the age of 20 they were elected to one of the *sussitia*, dining clubs or messes. Hence came the discipline for which the Spartans were famous. Every citizen was trained to be a soldier and lived constantly in a state of military preparedness. To a large extent, this state of affairs was a response to Sparta's own domestic situation. In the seventh century, she had overrun her neighbour Messenia and reduced her inhabitants to the status of Helots or serfs. The conquered land was distributed in an allotment, or *kleros*, to each Spartiate to be worked by the Helots, thus giving the citizens economic independence but also creating a permanent source of social tension, as the Spartiates lived in constant fear of an uprising from a population of Helots that greatly outnumbered the citizen body. This fear lead to the institution of a secret police force called the *krypteia*. Slavery existed throughout the Greek world, but no other Greek state was subject to actual revolt and the fear of revolt to such an extent. This fear dictated Sparta's foreign policy too. In the sixth century, she was involved in a war with her northern neighbour, Tegea. The defeated Tegeans were not treated like the Messenians, though they became dependent and were bound not to harbour Messenians within their borders. Sparta had a long rivalry with Argos, whom she also defeated in the sixth century. As the most powerful state in the Peloponnese, she now put herself at the head of the Peloponnesian League, a loose federation of states south of the isthmus (excluding Argos) in a largely defensive alliance who agreed to supply troops in common cause under Spartan leadership. Spartan policy thereafter was predominantly defensive; she was reluctant to dispatch significant numbers of her Spartiates north of the isthmus, for fear of revolt at home. The defensive atitude on the part of her ruling élite doubtless accounts for her more general cultural conservatism. In the seventh century Sparta had produced one of the most famous of early Greek poets, Tyrtaeus, who wrote war songs, and the choral lyric developed there, but at about the time that Athens was beginning to assert her cultural identity with new buildings, splendid festivals and beautiful pottery, Sparta was going in the opposite direction towards the life of simplicity and austerity to which she has given her name. By the time of the Persian Wars, the divergence between characteristic Spartan and Athenian values was already plain to see.

THE PERSIAN WARS

Sometime after 1000, Greeks from the mainland had migrated across the Aegean to settle on the coast of Asia Minor. These settlements had lived freely on peaceable terms with the unaggressive Lydian empire to their east. In 546, however, the Persians, who had already conquered the Medes, moved further west and their king, Cyrus, defeated Croesus, king of Lydia. Cyrus then annexed the Greek states. When in 499 the Ionian cities rose in revolt against Persian domination, they appealed to mainland Greeks for support. Only Athens and Eretria responded. In 498 they sent a force which together with the

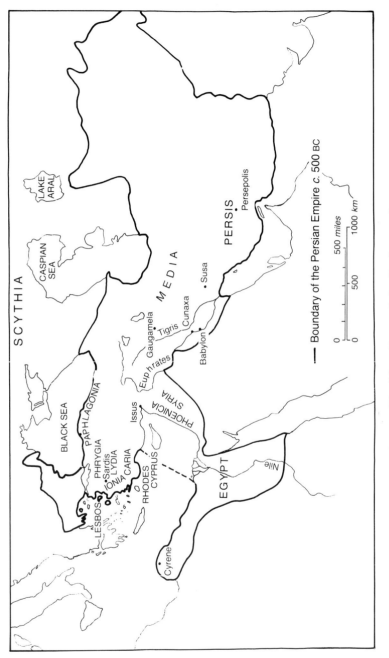

SCYTHIA

LAKE ARAL

CASPIAN SEA

BLACK SEA

PAPHLAGONIA

PHRYGIA

Sardis

LYDIA

IONIA

CARIA

LESBOS

RHODES

CYPRUS

Issus

PHOENICIA

SYRIA

Euphrates

Gaugamela

Tigris

Cunaxa

Babylon

M E D I A

Susa

PERSIS

Persepolis

EGYPT

Nile

Cyrene

— Boundary of the Persian Empire *c.* 500 BC

0   500   1000 km
0   500 miles

Figure 6   The Near East and the Persian empire

Ionians marched on Sardis, the former capital of Lydia; during their occupation, the city was burnt down. Herodotus tells us that when the Persian king learned of the disaster, he did not give a thought to the Ionians, knowing that their punishment would come. Instead, the first thing he did was to ask who the Athenians were. Then he commanded one of his servants to repeat to him the words 'Master, remember the Athenians' three times, whenever he sat down to dinner (V, 105).

The revolt was finally subdued in 494, and in 490 Darius mounted an expedition against the European Greeks, demanding from their cities the gifts of earth and water, tokens of submission. Most of the Greeks submitted except the Eretrians whose city was burnt and inhabitants enslaved. The Persians, accompanied by the exiled Athenian tyrant Hippias, now landed their army at the bay of Marathon. The Athenians, under the

Figure 7 The plain of Marathon (with the sea in the left-hand corner) and site of the battle, fought from left to right, with the Greeks in formation in the foothills and the Persians in the foreground. Athens is just over 26 miles to the west-south-west. Legend has it that the runner Pheidippides ran from Athens to join the battle, then ran back (the distance of the 'marathon') to deliver the news of the victory with the words 'Victory: we win', whereupon he dropped dead (*photograph: R. V. Schroder*)

generalship of Callimachus and Miltiades, marched out to meet them. The plan adopted was to face the Persian host, which greatly outnumbered the Greeks, with a long battle line weak at the centre and strong on the wings, in the hope of encircling the enemy as they broke through the centre. The plan worked and the Persian army was routed with losses reported to be well over 6,000 as against 192 Athenians. The Spartans, who had been celebrating a religious festival when requests for aid came to them from Athens, arrived with a force of 2,000, too late for the battle. The Persians returned home, abandoning their present expedition. In 487 the newly confident Athenian assembly used the provision of ostracism for the first time against Hipparchus, a descendant of the family of Peisistratus, now permanently tainted by their support for the Persian cause.

Preparations for a second and larger Persian expedition were made by Xerxes, the son of Darius, in the next decade. He had a vast army of perhaps 100,000 troops, including 10,000 specially trained 'Immortals' (so called because casualties in this division were immediately replaced to keep the numbers constant), accompanied by a fleet of perhaps 1,000 ships. He cut a canal across the isthmus of Mount Athos where an earlier Persian fleet had been shipwrecked. The Greeks held a congress at the Isthmus of Corinth where Sparta assumed the leadership. The first Greek resistance was made at the pass of Thermopylae in northern Greece where the Spartan king Leonidas was in command of a force of 6,000 men. He held the pass for several days until Xerxes sent the Immortals through the mountains with the intention of attacking the Greeks at the rear. When Leonidas had intelligence of this, he dismissed most of his force except for the 300 Spartans and contingents from Thespis and Thebes who were subsequently overwhelmed from front and rear. Herodotus records the epitaph composed for the Spartans by the poet Simonides:

> Stranger, go tell the Spartans that we lie here
> Obedient to their laws.

(VII, 228)

Their leader Themistocles now persuaded the Athenians to abandon their city, which at this time was not defended by walls. A far-sighted leader, he had earlier diverted money earned from a silver mine discovered at Laurium in Attica in the 480s to a fund for building up the Athenian fleet. He now persuaded the Athenians to trust to their ships and in all this laid the foundations of Athenian naval power, by which Athens came to dominate the Aegean. In the confrontation with Persia he prevented the Spartans from withdrawing the fleet south of the isthmus and opposed the Persians in the narrow waters off the island of Salamis, where their numerical superiority and the size of their ships proved to be a positive disadvantage. As at Marathon, intelligent tactics had triumphed over seemingly impossible odds. The battle of Salamis in 480 destroyed much of Xerxes' navy and he retired to Persia, leaving the army under the command of Mardonius. The Spartans were persuaded to oppose the Persians north of the isthmus and under their leader Pausanias won a famous victory in 479 at the battle of Plataea.

The Athenians now returned to Athens and Themistocles persuaded them to fortify their city and harbour. Later the building of long walls uniting the two, which were completed between 461 and 451, made the city invulnerable to attacks by land and fully able to capitalise upon her naval superiority.

The Persians retreated, but in the face of an obviously continuing threat, the states of the Aegean islands, the northern coast and Ionia came together on the sacred island of Delos, the birthplace of Apollo and Artemis, to form a voluntary league to which each member was to contribute annually either ships or an amount of money, to be supervised by Athenian officials called *Hellenotamiai*, treasurers of the Greeks. The league, which was the inspiration of the Athenian leader Aristides, also brought economic benefits by securing the main trading routes against piracy. In the early 460s, Cimon, the son of Miltiades, carried the campaign against Persia into Asia Minor and defeated the forces of Xerxes on land, and in 468 at the battle of Eurymedon in Pamphylia effectively eliminated the Persian threat. Cimon conducted further campaigns against Persian interests in Cyprus until his death in 460/59. Athens then resigned her claims to Cyprus in the Peace of Callias; both sides recognised each other's sphere of interest, and the supremacy of Athens in the Aegean was thereby confirmed.

HERODOTUS (*c.* 484–*c.* 420)

Born about 484, in between the two Persian campaigns, in

Halicarnassus, a colony of Dorian Greeks on the coast of Asia Minor, Herodotus offers to the public the result of his enquiry (for which the Greek word is *historia*) in order to preserve the memory and renown of great and remarkable deeds done both by the Greeks and the non-Greeks (for which his work is *barbaroi* meaning foreign but not necessarily uncivilised). More particularly he aims to show the reason why they came into conflict (I, 1). He then gives the Persian and Phoenician versions of the origin of eastern hostility to the Greeks, going back to the story of Io and the Trojan War. However, he quickly moves on from the mythical past:

> So much for what the Persians and Phoenicians say; and I have no intention of passing judgment on its truth or falsity. I prefer to rely on my own knowledge, and to point out what it was in actual fact that first injured the Greeks; then I will proceed with my history, telling the story as I go of small cities no less than of great. Most of those which were great are small today; and those which in my lifetime have grown to greatness were small enough in the old days. It makes no odds whether the cities I shall write of are big or little – for in this world nobody remains prosperous for long.
>
> (I, 5)

The stress here upon historical flux suggests the influence upon Herodotus of the physical speculations of the Ionian natural philosophers, especially Heraclitus. In actual fact, he finds the historical cause of the conflict to lie in the attack made by Croesus of Lydia upon the neighbouring empire of King Cyrus of Persia, in the course of which the Lydian empire, the buffer state between Persia and the Asiatic Greeks, was destroyed. He then gives the history of the eastern empire, concentrating upon the reign of Cyrus, who conquered first the Medes and then extended westwards by way of Lydia to the Asiatic Greeks. His successor Cambyses conquered Egypt; Darius and then Xerxes attempt the conquest of Europe. In the course of his account he tells us of the prevailing customs of each foreign people, notably the Lydians in Book One, the Persians in Books One and Three, the Egyptians in Book Two and the Scythians and Libyans in Book Four. He therefore gives us a history and description (geographical and ethnographical) of the whole of the Near East. As in the case of Homer, there are many episodes and

41

digressions, but essentially they are related and subordinated to one grand uniting theme. It is by virtue of this unity (reflecting the unity he saw in the human world), as well as the scale of the work and of course the interest in cause and effect, that Herodotus merits the title accorded to him in antiquity, 'the father of history', even though others had written history before him, and it is by virtue of his interest in different customs and peoples that he may also be called the father of anthropology and ethnology.

He acquired the material for his history sometimes from written records but usually from what he saw for himself or was told by those he met on his extensive travels. He lived for a time in Samos and at Athens, then after 444, for the last twenty years of his life, in the Athenian colony of Thurii in southern Italy. He tells us that he went to Egypt, to Gaza and Tyre, to Babylon, to Scythia and throughout the northern Aegean. In his addiction to travel (at a time when it was difficult and hazardous) and in his insatiable curiosity about men and manners, he can be likened in spirit to the Homeric Odysseus, and just as 'many-minded' Homer has respect for all his characters whether they are Greek or non-Greek, so Herodotus transcends his nationality in his tolerance, openness and sympathy, to the extent that he could later be criticised for being over-fond of the foreign, *philobarbaros*. He admires Egyptian achievements in medicine and philosophy, rightly regarding Egypt as the teacher of Greece. He admires, too, the courage and honesty of the enemies of Greece. The Persians are not simply seen as unciv-ilised hordes in the way that westerners have often seen, for example, the Turks. On national customs and beliefs he has the following instruction:

> Everyone without exception believes his own native customs, and the religion he was brought up in, to be the best. . . . One might recall, in particular, an anecdote of Darius. When he was king of Persia, he summoned the Greeks who happened to be present at his court, and asked them what they would take to eat the dead bodies of their fathers. They replied they would not do it for any money in the world. Later, in the presence of the Greeks, and through an interpreter so that they could understand what was said, he asked some Indians, of the tribe called Callatiae who do in

fact eat their parents' dead bodies, what they would take to burn them. They uttered a cry of horror and forbade him to mention such a dreadful thing. One can see by this what custom can do, and Pindar, in my opinion was right when he called it 'king of all'.

(III, 38)

If we are divided by custom, then in some fundamental respects all men are equal: 'I am not anxious to repeat what I was told about the Egyptian religion apart from the mere names of the deities, for I do not think any one nation knows more about such things than any other' (II, 3).

It will follow from this that Herodotus does not write in the belief that the Greeks are the chosen people of the gods whose victory is divinely ordained. Greek history, recognising a universal pattern of rise and fall, is not teleological on the Jewish pattern. On the other hand, Herodotus does clearly believe that the gods do intervene in human affairs. Recording the view of Egyptian priests that Helen and the treasure at Sparta stolen by Paris had been removed to Egypt and that the Greeks did not believe the Trojan account, and dismissing the implausibility of the Homeric version in which the Trojans refuse to surrender Helen, he adds his own view:

> The fact is, they did not give Helen up because they had not got her; what they told the Greeks was the truth, and I do not hesitate to declare that the refusal of the Greeks to believe it was inspired by providence, in order that their utter destruction might plainly prove to mankind that sin is always visited by condign punishment at the hands of god. That at least is my own belief.

> (II, 120)

Similarly he accepts the validity of oracles: 'Now I cannot deny that there is truth in prophecies, and I have no wish to discredit them, when they are expressed in unambiguous language' (VIII, 77). In the case of the famous oracle given to the Athenians at Delphi that in the face of the Persians they should trust to 'their wooden walls', while the narrative is designed to show the political wisdom of Themistocles in his interpretation that the Athenians should trust to their ships, there is no hint of incredulity or cynicism about the institution of the Delphic oracle itself (which continued to be a potent force in the Greek world down to Hellenistic times). Omens and prophetic dreams (notably in the case of Xerxes (VII, 13)) also play a part in his history. Nevertheless, Herodotus never takes upon himself the role of prophet, nor do the gods intervene crudely in his history of the Persians Wars in such a way as to compromise the exercise of human free will.

What Herodotus believed about the intervention of the gods in history may be discerned in the tale in which the wise Greek Solon advises the rich Lydian ruler Croesus who supposed himself the happiest of men: 'Look to the end, no matter what you are considering. Often enough god gives a man a glimpse of happiness, and then utterly ruins him' (I, 32). Croesus thinks Solon a fool. 'After Solon's departure Croesus was dreadfully punished, presumably because god was angry with him for supposing himself the happiest of men' (I, 33–4). The fate of Croesus is an object lesson in the folly of over-confidence and pride, as the advice of Solon, very much in the spirit of Herodotus, expresses the Greek fear of excess. Here we have one of the leading ideas that shaped Herodotus' interpretation of events, that of *hybris* inevitably begetting a corresponding *nemesis* in individuals and states. While he gives us finely individualised portraits of the four great Persian kings, who all have some qualities he admires, the Persian invasion is a manifestation of *hybris*, particularly on the part of Xerxes, whose character expresses the arrogance of power. Similarly, the tragic dramatist Aeschylus in his play the *Persians* has the ghost of Darius say that Xerxes' *hybris* was punished by the gods 'who used the rashness of his nature against him' (ll. 742–4). When the king orders his men to lash the Hellespont, throw fetters into it, brand it with irons and utter curses over it after a storm has destroyed a recently constructed bridge, Herodotus remarks on the presumptuous folly of this 'barbarous' behaviour, and here for once the word has a special charge (VII, 35). There soon follows a story that needs no comment in which the Lydian Pythius requests Xerxes to allow his eldest son to remain with him in his old age. Xerxes angrily orders that the son be cut in half so that the army can march between the two halves (VII, 39). In conversation with the exiled Spartan king Demaratus, Herodotus shows not only the understandable incomprehension of Xerxes when told that the Spartans will fight him whatever the odds but also betrays the king's inability to appreciate that strength and discipline might be induced by anything other than the tyranny of the lash:

> If, like ours, the troops were subject to the control of a single man, then possibly for fear of him in spite of the disparity in numbers, they might show some sort of factitious courage, or let themselves be whipped into battle; but as every man is free to follow his fancy, it is inconceivable that they should do either.
>
> (VII, 103)

Demaratus seeks to enlighten him:

> They are free – yes – but not entirely free, for they have a master and that master is law, which they fear as much as your subjects fear you. Whatever that master commands, they do; and his command never varies; it is never to retreat in battle, however great the odds, but always to stand firm, and to conquer or to die.
>
> (VII, 104)

Unlike Xerxes, Herodotus appreciates the value of freedom. Commenting on Athenian military success after the expulsion of the tyrants, he writes:

> Thus Athens went from strength to strength, and proved, if proof were needed, how noble a thing freedom is, not in one respect only but in all; for while they were oppressed under a despotic government, they had no better success in war than any of their neighbours yet, once the yoke was flung off, they proved the finest fighters in the world. This clearly shows that, so long as they were held down by authority, they deliberately shirked their duty in the field, as slaves shirk working for masters; but when freedom was won, then every man amongst them longed to distinguish himself.
>
> (V, 78)

In the debate between leading Persians on the best form of constitution, whether democracy, oligarchy or monarchy, the critique of monarchy and the ideal of democracy stand out (though elsewhere he is not uncritical of democratic practice):

> Contrast with this the rule of the people: first it has the finest

of all names to describe it – *isonomy* or equality before the law; and secondly the people in power do none of the things that monarchs do. Under the government of the people a magistrate is appointed by lot and is held responsible for his conduct in office, and all questions are put up for open debate.

(III, 80)

Though not an Athenian himself and evidently writing at a time when Athens was unpopular as a result of her empire, Herodotus boldly hails freedom-loving Athens as the saviour of Greece: Athenian naval power was decisive. 'It was Athens too who, after the gods, drove back the Persian king' (VII, 138). *Philobarbaros* though he certainly is, Herodotus has no doubt that Greek civic values represent a higher order of things than oriental despotism, and his history expresses the new self-confidence in Greece in the generation after the Persian Wars.

Most readers find his history an attractively written and fascinating human document which rises to a dramatic climax in the two Persian campaigns, but the reliability of it all has always been a matter of debate. The narrative of Solon and Croesus (I, 29–34) sounds like a folk-tale and even in ancient times was rejected on chronological grounds. We may suspect that the conversations between Xerxes and Demaratus and the discussion on the various forms of constitution are largely if not wholly invented for dramatic effect, though here it can be said in Herodotus' defence that it remained the general practice of ancient historians to put words into the mouths of their protagonists. He is often criticised not only for lapses in chronology but also for a lack of military knowledge and often for a general credulity in relation to his sources. But it would be wrong simply to regard the history as largely a compilation of travellers' tales preserving the distorted folk memories of the oral tradition, followed by a dramatic account of the Persian Wars in which historical truth is often sacrificed for literary effect. He frequently expresses scepticism about what he is told and sometimes gives two versions of events, leaving the reader to decide the balance of probability. Modern scholars who have looked beyond Herodotus to the evidence of inscriptions and archaeology often report back with favourable verdicts. Given the difficulties in writing history at all in an age when written records were not available, and in determining criteria for deciding between myth and fact, and given that Herodotus is a pioneer in the scale of his undertaking, it is difficult not to admire the lengths to which he went in his pursuit of truth about the human world of his recent past.

DEMOCRACY AND EMPIRE: PERICLEAN ATHENS

As a result of the policy of Themistocles and successes in the Persian Wars, Athens became a fully fortified city and a strong naval power. The Delian League organised by Aristides further extended Athenian influence. When the island of Naxos attempted to secede from the league in 470, it was prevented from doing so, forfeiting its fleet and its defensive walls and being required to contribute money, which was spent upon the Athenian navy. In 465 the island of Thasos also attempted to secede and met a similar fate. Gradually fewer states contributed ships and more contributed money which was obviously to the Athenian advantage. Individual cities made their own arrangements with the leading power, but there is evidence that Athens interfered with the constitutions of member states, favouring more democratic arrangements, so that initially the federation was united by the need not only to combat an external threat but also perhaps to secure democratic constitutions against their oligarchic predecessors. At any rate, by the time that the treasury of the league was moved from Delos to Athens in 454, it was clear to all that what had begun as a voluntary association had gradually become the empire of Athens.

The empire, secured by the navy, was centred upon the Aegean and the maritime states of northern and western Greece. Spartan power, secured by the Spartiate army (Sparta had only a small navy and little naval expertise), was centred upon the Peloponnesian League, a loose non-tributary federation of all states south of the isthmus of Corinth except Argos (an age-old rival) and Achaea. Sparta also had alliances with states such as Thebes north of the isthmus. The policy of the Athenian democracy in mid-century was expansionist, and her ambitions on land brought Athens into conflict with Sparta. In 460 Athens made an alliance with Argos and in 459, Megara, strategically situated on the northern side of the isthmus of Corinth, withdrew from the Peloponnesian League to make an alliance with

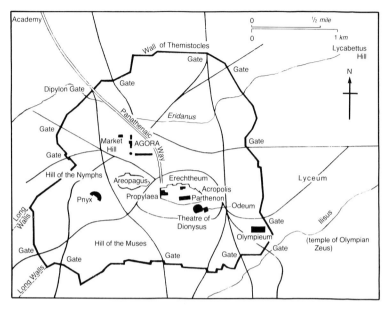

Figure 8a Athens

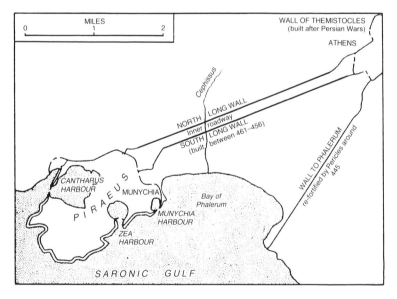

Figure 8b Piraeus and the Long Walls

48

Athens. The Athenians intervened in conflicts between states north of the isthmus, but did not have the military means to sustain their power on land, so that, after fifteen years of intermittent hostilities, the Thirty Year Peace treaty was signed between Sparta and Athens in 446, in which Athens gave up her ambitions on land in return for Spartan recognition of Athenian naval hegemony.

Internal changes had taken place in Athens since the constitution of Cleisthenes. In 487, it was decided that the archons should subsequently be elected by lot, one from each of the ten tribes, from 500 candidates nominated by the demes and selected not exclusively from the first class of citizens but including the second class too. Thus the power of the old aristocratic families was severely curtailed. In 454 the archonship was opened up to the third class of citizens. This further weakened the power of the wealthiest and broadened the democratic base of the state. In 462–461 Ephialtes, supported by Pericles, reduced the privileges and powers of the Areopagus, a body composed of ex-archons who held office for life (a majority of whom were likely to be aristocratic or wealthy), which had general guardianship of the constitution. Jurisdiction over all cases except those involving homicide was transferred to the popular courts, the Heliaea, so that the people virtually monopolised the administration of justice. Other powers were transferred to the council, making the role of the Areopagus largely ceremonial. Pericles then introduced payment for jury service. Thereafter payment for office which might encourage the less wealthy became a feature of the radical democracy.

In the developed democracy, the sovereign body was the assembly (the *ekklesia*), of which all adult male citizens were members. Business was put before it, in the form of motions, by the council of 500 (the *boule*), to which appointment was by lot from those over 30. No one could serve on the council more than twice in a lifetime. The Athenian year was split into ten parts of 36 days each called a prytany. The council was also subdivided into ten groups of 50 which each presided for a prytany. This was a small enough group to pay, and its members met every day. There were four assemblies per prytany. One was required to take a vote of confidence on the officials then serving, to oversee arrangements for the corn supply and for the defence of the state. At another meeting, petitioners could address the people formally on any subject. The remaining meetings were for other business. The meeting place for the assembly was on the lower slopes of a small hill called the Pnyx near the Agora and the Acropolis, and may have accommodated as many as 6,000, though we may suppose that numbers were generally much lower. Meetings were begun with the question 'who wishes to speak to the assembly?' In theory any citizen might take up the challenge. Voting seems to have been chiefly by a show of hands. The assembly's decisions were implemented by the council, which also had an important role in financial matters. Only those officers whose duties required special expertise, such as the ten generals or certain financial administrators, were not appointed by lot but by annual election with prior nomination. The generals could be re-elected annually. But all officials had to undergo scrutiny before taking office and were accountable upon leaving it. The cornerstones of the developed democracy were therefore sortition (also a feature of the lawcourts with their mass juries) and rotation, which prevented power being concentrated in factions or individual office-holders.

During the period between 463 (and particularly after 447) and his death in 429, the most influential figure in Athens was Pericles, who has lent his name to the whole era, which is regarded as the high-water mark of Athenian power and influence. Though born into the aristocracy and nicknamed the Olympian because of the aloofness of his bearing and manner, he encouraged and initiated democratic reforms. His power stemmed from his ability to control the assembly by virtue of his oratory. He was elected general several times and from 443, after the ostracism of an opponent, on an annual basis until his death. In 447 he called a Panhellenic congress, proposing the rebuilding of the temples destroyed by the Persians, freedom of the seas and a general peace. In this he was thwarted by Spartan opposition. In 446 he negotiated the Thirty Years Peace in which Sparta recognised Athenian naval hegemony. He put down attempts by Euboea and Samos to secede from the league in 446 and 440, and supported the policy of strengthening the empire by establishing colonies in some existing states. In 437 he himself established a colony at Amphipolis in northern Greece. Shortly afterwards he extended Athenian influence in the region of the Hellespont. After the outbreak of the Peloponnesian War, which he favoured at the time and for which he had worked out a strategy, Thucydides represents his thoughts on the Athenian empire as follows:

> Then it is right and proper for you to support the imperial dignity of Athens. This is something in which you all take pride, and you cannot continue to enjoy the privileges unless you also shoulder the burdens of empire. . . . Your empire is now like a tyranny: it may have been wrong to take it; it is certainly dangerous to let it go.
>
> (II, 63)

A successful general, politician and orator, Pericles was a cultivated man who numbered among his friends the philosopher Anaxagoras, the playwright Sophocles and the sculptor Pheidias. In his time Athens became the cultural centre of the Greek world and the home of visiting intellectuals and artists in all fields. In Periclean Athens, Socrates began his philosophic mission. A grand programme of public building was initiated with Periclean support and under the general control of Pheidias. Included in this was Athens' most famous building, the Parthenon, the temple of Athena Parthenos (meaning 'maiden') situated on the Acropolis which was begun in 447 and completed in 432. In the course of one of the most famous speeches of its kind, the funeral oration over the Athenian dead in the first year of the war with Sparta in 430, Pericles, in Thucydides' words, gives voice to the ideals of his age, stressing the value of the democratic constitution, equality before the law, the absolute recognition of merit, the commercial and cultural pre-eminence of Athens, the love of beauty and philosophy, and the dedication of the individual to the community.

> Taking everything together then, I declare that our city is an education to Greece, and I declare that in my opinion each single one of our citizens, in all the manifold aspects of life, is able to show himself the rightful lord and owner of his own person, and do this moreover, with exceptional grace and exceptional versatility.
>
> (II, 41)

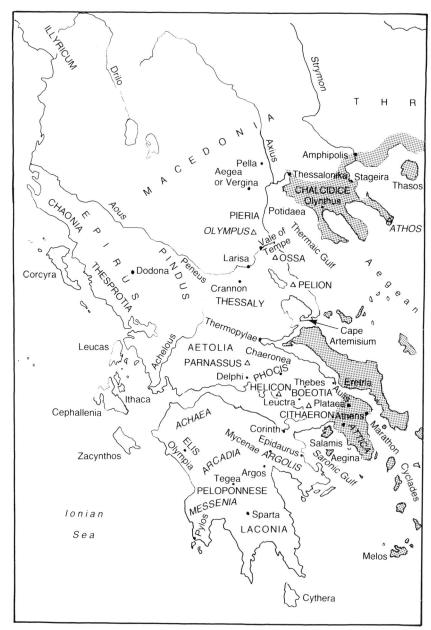

Figure 9 The Greek world in the classical era showing the Athenian empire in the second half of the 5th century

Euxine
(Black Sea)

Bosporus

A   C   E

Byzantium

Chalcedon

Propontis
(*Sea of Marmora*)

B I T H Y N I A

Abdera

THRACIAN
CHERSONESE

Aegospotami

M Y S I A

Imbros

Lemnos   Hellespont   *Sigeum*

P H R Y G I A

Tenedos   *Troy*   THE TROAD   △ IDA

Assos

A E O L I S

Mitylene   Pergamum

Lesbos   L Y D I A

Arginusae

Sea

Hermus

Sardis

Smyrna   *Pactolus*

Chios

Maeander

O

Samos   Ephesus

Delos

Miletus   C A R I A

Sporades

Naxos

A

Halicarnassus

Cos   L Y C I A

Cnidus

Rhodes

Rhodes

THE PELOPONNESIAN WAR

The immediate occasion of this major conflict, which was fought out in various phases from the outbreak of hostilities in 431 until the defeat of Athens in 404, was a dispute between Athens and Corinth over Corcyra, a colony of the latter which sought to make an alliance with Athens contrary to the interests of Corinth, which appealed to Sparta to intervene. Sparta declared war with the expressed aim of liberating the states of Greece from the dominance of Athens. Thucydides, the historian of the war, finds the underlying cause to be Spartan fear of increasing Athenian power (I, 23).

The strategy of Pericles was to avoid a pitched battle with the superior Spartan forces by retreating behind the walls by which the city and the harbour were both connected and defended. With naval superiority, Athens was assured of food supplies by way of her traditional corn routes through the Bosporus. Meanwhile she might herself blockade the Peloponnese, interfering with food imports and sowing dissension among the allies of Sparta. When the Spartans invaded Attica, which they did in the corn-growing season for the first six years of war, the rural population retreated to the city. One of the most promising engagements from the Athenian point of view was the occupation of Pylos in Messenia on the eastern coast of the Peloponnese. Here a number of Spartiates were taken prisoner and shipped back to Athens, and from here it might have been expected that the Athenians could foment a rebellion of the Messenian Helots. Sparta sued for peace but the successors of Pericles (who had died in 429) urged continuation of the war. Sparta now made a successful attempt against the Athenian empire in the north, in the Thracian Chalcidice, where she captured Amphipolis, an important source of raw materials and a promising base for further interference in the region. But neither side could press home any significant advantage in the overall conflict, and a peace was agreed in 421 in which both sides more or less gave up their gains and returned to the status quo. Athenian power remained intact.

The peace did not suit the allies of Sparta, and Athens, at the instigation of Alcibiades who had been brought up in the household of Pericles and now began to dominate the assembly, exploited discontent by making alliances with Peloponnesian

states in dispute with Sparta, who reasserted her dominance at
the battle of Mantinea in 418. Athens subjugated the island of
Melos, one of the few states not subject to her in the Aegean,
putting to death all men of military age and selling the women
and children into slavery. In 415 envoys from Egesta in Sicily
came to Athens requiring aid in a Sicilian war. According to
Thucydides (II, 65) Pericles had advised the Athenians not to
extend their empire during their conflict with Sparta. The
general Nicias, who had negotiated the peace in 421, was
against intervention but Alcibiades' enthusiastic support won
the day and the Athenians mounted a huge expedition, doubtless
with the aim of extending the empire. Alcibiades was recalled to
Athens to answer charges of sacrilegious behaviour, whereupon
he fled to Sparta and proceeded to help the enemy. The fleet,
despite being heavily reinforced, was defeated and destroyed,
and the troops were taken prisoner after a two-year campaign in
413. This was the decisive event of the war, which weakened
Athenian power, with the loss of a huge fleet and perhaps over
40,000 men. It was a blow from which Athens never recovered.

At the suggestion of Alcibiades, the Spartans had by now
established a permanent base at Decelea in Attica, restricting
Athenian movement by land. Taking advantage of Athenian
weakness, a number of states in her empire revolted, while
Sparta began to equip herself with a new fleet for war in the
Aegean. Athens now made the mistake of involving Persia in the
war by supporting the revolt of Amorge in Caria against Persian
rule. As a result, Persia gave financial support to Sparta, for a
Spartan victory would result in increased Persian influence in an
Asia Minor deprived of Athenian protection. Sparta and Persia
made a treaty in which the Spartans acknowledged the Persian
king's right to sovereignty over the Asiatic Greeks in return for
Persian support. Persian gold was a decisive factor in the
eventual Spartan victory. Athens in the meantime was running
out of funds and her supplies of corn from the Bosporus were
threatened by the new Peloponnesian fleet. Alcibiades, now in
Persia, made contact with the Athenian fleet at Samos, promising to arrange for Persia to change sides if the Athenian leaders
in return overthrew the democratic constitution. An oligarchic
revolution took place in 411 establishing government by a body
of 400. The oligarchs did not succeed in bringing peace with
Sparta and the constitution was modified to a more moderate

oligarchy, giving rights to the 5,000 or so most wealthy citizens. In the following year, 410, radical democracy was restored.

Alcibiades had now been recalled and with a new fleet he successfully secured the corn supplies, restoring Athenian power in much of the Aegean. At the battle of Arginusae in 406 the Athenians defeated the Spartan fleet, but lost many ships and men in a subsequent storm. All the victorious generals were tried and executed on their return to Athens. An offer of peace was also spurned. The much-reduced Athenian fleet was finally defeated at the battle of Aegospotami in the Hellespont. With no fleet to protect her and besieged by land, Athens capitulated in 404. Sparta required her to dismantle her long walls and the fortifications of the Piraeus, to maintain a fleet of no more than twelve ships and to recall citizens exiled when the earlier oligarchy had been overthrown. An oligarchic coup with Spartan support followed. A board of thirty took over and began a reign of terror against their political opponents. Leading democrats who had escaped to Thebes then returned, occupied the Piraeus and fought the Thirty, killing a number of them. The Spartans did not then oppose the gradual restoration of democratic government.

THUCYDIDES (c. 455–c. 400)

The chief source for the Peloponnesian War and one of the greatest of Greek writers is Thucydides:

> I lived through the whole of it, being of an age to understand what was happening, and I put my mind to the subject so as to get an accurate view of it. It happened, too, that I was banished from my country for twenty years after my command at Amphipolis; I saw what was being done on both sides, particularly on the Peloponnesian side, because of my exile, and this leisure gave me rather exceptional facilities for looking into things.
>
> (V, 26)

In the event, he did not complete the history, finishing in mid-sentence in 411. The event referred to here, when, as Athenian general, he lost Amphipolis in 423 to the Spartan Brasidas is narrated stoically at IV, 103–8. It is supposed that he was in exile until the end of the war. The Athenian assembly, which later ordered the execution of all surviving generals after Arginusae in 406, was always likely to deal harshly with those who did not deliver success. Even Pericles had been fined in the last year of his life (II, 65). Little of Thucydides' life is known apart from what he tells us himself, but he was from an aristocratic family and his own political inclinations may be inferred from his comment on the government of the Five Thousand: 'Indeed, during the first period of this new regime the Athenians appear to have had a better government than ever before, at least in my time. There was a reasonable and moderate blending of the few and the many' (VIII, 97). He was a great admirer of Pericles and in the following chapter (II, 65), written after the downfall of Athens, he offers a summary analysis of its downfall:

Indeed, during the whole period of peace-time when Pericles was at the head of affairs the state was wisely led and firmly guarded, and it was under him that Athens was at her greatest. And when the war broke out, here, too, he appears to have accurately estimated what the power of Athens was . . . . For Pericles had said that Athens would be victorious if she bided her time and took care of her navy, if she avoided trying to add to the empire during the course of the war, and if she did nothing to risk the safety of the city itself. But his successors did the exact opposite, and in other matters which apparently had no connection with the war private ambition and private profit led to policies which were bad for both the Athenians themselves and for their allies. Such policies, when successful, only brought credit and advantage to individuals, and when they failed, the whole war potential of the state was impaired. The reason for this was that Pericles, because of his position, his intelligence, and his known integrity, could respect the liberty of the people and at the same time hold them in check. It was he who led them, rather than they who led him, and since he never sought power from any wrong motive, he was under no necessity of flattering them: in fact he was so highly res- pected that he was able to speak angrily to them and to contradict them. Certainly when he saw that they were going too far in a mood of over-confidence, he would bring back to them a sense of their dangers; and when they were discouraged for no good reason he would restore their confidence. So, in what was nominally a democracy, power was really in the hands of the first citizen. But his successors, who were more on a level with each other and each of whom aimed at occupying the first place, adopted methods of demagogy which resulted in their losing control over the actual conduct of affairs. Such a policy, in a great city with an empire to govern, naturally led to a number of mistakes, amongst which was the Sicilian expedition, though in this case the mistake was not so much an error of judgement with regard to the opposition to be expected as a failure on the part of those who were at home to give proper support to their forces overseas. Because they were so busy with their own personal intrigues for securing the leadership of the people, they allowed this expedition to lose its impetus, and by quarrelling among themselves began to bring confusion into the policy of the state.

In his criticism of the successors of Pericles he has been judged to have been hard on Cleon. Some historians have felt that his own narrative of events belies his judgement that the Sicilian expedition was not properly supported. Nevertheless, even those who disagree with his analysis generally accord to Thucydides more respect than to any other ancient historian.

Like Herodotus, he relied chiefly on oral sources and, unlike Herodotus, he did not have the disadvantage of often dealing with long-forgotten events. In the comparison between the two great historians that has often been made, Thucydides has always been regarded as the more scientific, the more accurate and reliable in matters of chronology and fact, and the more questioning and searching in his powers of analysis, whether that be in sifting the evidence of his sources, or in coming to conclusions about motives and underlying causes. Moreover, unlike Herodotus, Thucydides, the rationalist, regarded the historical process as an entirely human affair and excluded the divine from his account, though he recognised, of course, the influence played by belief in the divine upon human events, as in the case of the failure of the Athenian general Nicias, 'who was rather over-inclined to divination and such things' (VII, 50), to make a politic retreat at a crucial junction in the Sicilian campaign because of an eclipse of the moon. He is seen at his scientific best in his clinical description of the plague (which he caught himself) in the second year of the war (II, 47–54), which he sees not as a divine judgement but as an unforseen event with greatly demoralising psychological effects. The uncrowned gods in Thucydides' narrative are chance and the unforeseen.

His scientific method is to serve a scientific purpose:

> And it may well be that my history will seem less easy to read because of the absence in it of a romantic element [*to mythodes*: perhaps he has Herodotus in mind here]. It will be enough for me, however, if these words of mine are judged useful by those who want to understand clearly the events which happened in the past and which (human nature being what it is) will, at some time or other and in much the same way, be repeated in the future. My work is not a piece of writing designed to meet the taste of an immediate public, but was done to last for ever.
>
> (I, 22)

He therefore writes with the lessons of history in mind, hoping to provide a useful education in political behaviour in the belief not so much that history repeats itself as that human nature always remains the same. There is every reason to believe that he would have disagreed with the later formulation of the philosopher Aristotle on the difference between poetry and history:

> the one tells of what has happened, the other of the kind of things that might happen. For this reason poetry is something more philosophical and more worthy of serious attention than history: for while poetry is concerned with universal truths, history treats only particular facts.
>
> (*Poetics*, IX)

Thucydides tells us what happened in such a way that we may see what might happen in the future given the human condition.

It is in the light of this that we may interpret the seemingly unscientific practice that he shares with Herodotus in the composition of his speeches:

> I have found it difficult to remember the precise words used in the speeches which I listened to myself and my various informants have experienced the same difficulty; so my method has been, while keeping as closely as possible to

the general sense of the words actually used, to make the speakers say what in my opinion, was called for by each situation.

(I, 22)

Most readers probably feel that there is more of Thucydides than of actual historical reality in these speeches. In the narrative of events Thucydides rarely intervenes with interpretive comment; in what is often a plain style he endeavours to tell us straightforwardly what happened. The narrative is complemented by speeches written in a quite different style, more abstract and condensed, in which issues and motives are explored. For example, he does not intervene in the narrative to define the different characteristics of the leading protagonists; instead he puts the characterisation (explored further in the funeral oration of Pericles) in the speech of the Corinthian envoy to Sparta at the beginning of the war:

> An Athenian is always an innovator, quick to form a resolution and quick at carrying it out. You, on the other hand, are good at keeping things as they are; you never originate an idea, and your action tends to stop short of its aim. Then again, Athenian daring will outrun its own resources; they will take risks against their better judgement, and still, in the midst of danger, remain confident. But your nature is always to do less than you could have done, to mistrust your own judgement, however sound it may be, and to assume that dangers will last for ever. Think of this, too: while you are hanging back, they never hesitate; while you stay at home, they are always abroad; for they think that the farther they go the more they will get, while you think that any movement may endanger what you have already. If they win a victory, they follow it up at once, and if they suffer a defeat, they scarcely fall back at all. As for their bodies, they regard them as expendable for their city's sake, as though they were not their own; but each man cultivates his own intelligence, again with a view to doing something notable for his city. If they aim at something and do not get it, they think that they have been deprived of what belonged to them already; whereas, if their enterprise is successful, they regard that success as nothing compared to what they will do next. Suppose they fail in some undertaking; they make good

the loss immediately by setting their hopes in some other direction. Of them alone it may be said that they possess a thing almost as soon as they have begun to desire it, so quickly with them does action follow upon decision. And so they go on working away in hardship and danger all the days of their lives, seldom enjoying their possessions because they are always adding to them. Their view of a holiday is to do what needs doing; they prefer hardship and activity to peace and quiet. In a word, they are by nature incapable of either living a quiet life themselves or of allowing anyone else to do so.

(I, 70)

The speeches, therefore, have dramatic effect, and to some extent fulfil an artistic function in bringing the whole conflict to life. But they are also scientific; for in them is included the main burden of the political (and sometimes military and social) analysis. In the debate, for example, between Cleon and Diodotus on the fate of the inhabitants of Mitylene (III, 9–14) or in the Melian dialogue (V, 85–113), Thucydides starkly dramatises the calculations of those who are impervious to any considerations other than their own self-interested power. We are forced to draw our own conclusions.

Occasionally he intervenes directly (as in II, 65 on p. 57, above) with analytical comment, and the most celebrated occasion is the extended analysis, prompted by the revolution in Corcyra, of civil war, or party strife, or faction, all of which are contained in the Greek word *stasis*. An extract is given here to illustrate the way in which Thucydides' probing moral insight, working upon the events of his own time and his own experience, is directed towards the identification of universal traits in human behaviour:

> In the various cities these revolutions were the cause of many calamities – as happens and always will happen while human nature is what it is, though there may be different degrees of savagery, and, as different circumstances arise, the general rules will admit of some variety. In times of peace and prosperity cities and individuals alike follow higher standards, because they are not forced into a situation where they have to do what they do not want to do. But war is a stern teacher; in depriving them of the power of easily satisfying their daily wants, it brings most people's

minds down to the level of their actual circumstances.

So revolutions broke out in city after city, and in places where the revolutions occurred late the knowledge of what had happened previously in other places caused still new extravagances of revolutionary zeal, expressed by an elaboration in the methods of seizing power and by unheard-of atrocities in revenge. To fit in with the change of events, words, too, had to change their usual meanings. What used to be described as a thoughtless act of aggression was now regarded as the courage one would expect to find in a party member; to think of the future and wait was merely another way of saying one was a coward; any idea of moderation was just an attempt to disguise one's unmanly character; ability to understand a question from all sides meant that one was totally unfitted for action. Fanatical enthusiasm was the mark of a real man, and to plot against an enemy was perfectly legitimate self-defence. Anyone who held violent opinions could always be trusted, and anyone who objected to them became a suspect . . . . Certainly it was in Corcyra that there occurred the first examples of the breakdown of law and order. There was the revenge taken in their hour of triumph by those who had in the past been arrogantly oppressed instead of wisely governed; there were the wicked resolutions taken by those who, particularly under the pressure of misfortune, wished to escape from their usual poverty and coveted the property of their neighbours; there were the savage and pitiless actions into which men were carried not so much for the sake of gain as because they were swept away into an internecine struggle by their ungovernable passions. Then, with the ordinary conventions of civilized life thrown into confusion, human nature, always ready to offend even where laws exist, showed itself proudly in its true colours, as something incapable of controlling passion, insubordinate to the idea of justice, the enemy to anything superior to itself; for, if it had not been for the pernicious power of envy, men would not so have exalted vengeance above innocence and profit above justice. Indeed, it is true that in these acts of revenge on others men take it upon themselves to begin the process of repealing those general laws of humanity which are there to give a hope of salvation to all who are in distress, instead of leaving those laws in existence, remembering that there may come a time when they, too, will be in danger and will need their protection.

(III, 82–5)

Thucydides is hard-headed in the determination of fact and rigorous in his political analysis. His history is also written with great imaginative power and dramatic intensity, evidenced especially in the account of the Sicilian disaster in Books Six and Seven. Herodotus had celebrated the triumph of Greece in which Athens had played a leading role. Thucydides shows us Athens in a decline and fall from greatness, the tyrant city betrayed by various forms of excess into overreaching itself with tragic consequences. Beneath the surface of the narrative this undercurrent of tragic feeling gives shape to the whole.

SPARTAN HEGEMONY AND THE SECOND ATHENIAN LEAGUE

Sparta now inherited the Athenian empire and was the undisputed leader of the Greek world. In spite of her declared aim to free the Greek states from the tyranny of Athens, she proceeded to substitute one form of control for another which was even more resented, since she established oligarchic governments of ten men supported by a military presence in a number of key states. The imperialism of Sparta appears to have been considerably less enlightened than that of Athens in her heyday. Nor were her foreign relations more wisely pursued, for she lost the crucial support of Persia (without which she could never have defeated Athens) when she supported the unsuccessful revolt of Cyrus, the younger brother of the Persian king, Artaxerxes. Cyrus' army included a number of Greek mercenaries (over 10,000). They marched from Sardis near the coast of Asia Minor to the confluence of the Euphrates and the Tigris, where they defeated the troops of Artaxerxes, who had marched west from the Persian capital, Susa, to meet them. But when Cyrus himself was killed, the whole purpose of the expedition was lost. This campaign and the long march back of the Ten Thousand is recorded by the Athenian Xenophon, who took part in it and became general in its later stages. The safe return of the Greeks after their long march was a tribute to their discipline and

63

purpose, but also led to a new view of the weakness of the Persians, who had not prevented it. At Cyrus' instigation, the Greek cities of Asia Minor had revolted from Persian control and received Greek garrisons. Under threat, the Asiatic Greeks appealed to Sparta for protection, so that Sparta became embroiled in war with Persia. She took the war into the interior of Asia Minor, but lost her fleet in a naval engagement with the Persians and the Athenian mercenary Conon in 394. The Persians proceeded to expel all Spartan garrisons from the Aegean, then, persuaded by Conon, helped the Athenians to rebuild their walls. In 389 the Athenian fleet sailed to the Hellespont and established Athens' old imperial alliances in the northern Aegean. This, however, was not in Persian interests, and Sparta succeeded in turning the Persian king against his Greek allies. In 387/6, Sparta imposed upon the Greek world the King's Peace, which she had devised and which had been approved and dictated by the king. The cities in Asia Minor were to be the king's; in return he agreed to let the rest of the Greek states be autonomous.

> The King has indeed achieved something which is beyond the achievements of all his ancestors. He has secured the admission from both Athens and Sparta that Asia belongs to him, and has assumed such authoritative control of the Greek cities there as either to raze them to the ground, or build fortifications in them. And all this is due to our folly, not to his power.

So wrote the rhetorician and teacher Isocrates in his *Panegyricus* of 380 (137), in which he advocated a Panhellenic response to the Persians and put forward Athenian claims to the joint leadership of Greece.

Sparta's position as a leading Greek power, however, was increasingly under threat. In 378, with Theban support, Athens established a second league. Seventy states joined this league in what was represented as an anti-Spartan alliance. Thebes, asserting her power in central Greece, gained a famous victory against the Spartans at the battle of Leuctra in Boeotia in 371, which finally confined Sparta to the Peloponnese which she found increasingly difficult to control. The Spartans never recovered their dominant position in the affairs of Greece. Athens meanwhile reverted to her old imperial ways, demanding contributions to the league treasury, using the fleet for her own purposes and refusing the right of secession, until in 357 a concerted revolt caused the collapse of the league after a two-year conflict in 355.

Greece had now reverted to its essentially fragmented state; the individual city states, perpetually at war with one another and competing for power, could devise no kind of permanent alliance for their common good. They were therefore an easy prey for the new Macedonian power developing to the north under the direction of King Philip II.

THE RISE OF PHILIP OF MACEDON

After his accession to the throne in 359, Philip gradually secured his power base in Macedonia, moved against neighbouring tribes in Thrace, Paeonia and Illyria in the east, north and west, and in 357 gained control of the strategic coastal city of Amphipolis, formerly part of the old Athenian empire and still an object of Athenian ambitions. After further victories against his non-Greek neighbours, the now undisputed strongman of the north was invited by the Thessalians to assist them in a conflict against their southern neighbours. Victory here in 352 established his power and extended his influence in Greece. He had further victories in Thrace and then in 349 moved against his former allies in the Chalcidice, whereupon Olynthus, its leading city, sought an alliance with Athens. Despite Athenian help, Olynthus was razed to the ground and its inhabitants enslaved in 348. Athens was preoccupied with the revolt of Euboea and unable to devote her dwindling resources to deal with the threat to her interests in the northern Aegean. The Peace of Philocrates (named after one of the Athenian negotiators) was concluded in 346 on the basis that Athens and Macedonia should retain the territories of which each was in possession. With the exception of the Thracian Chersonese, Philip now controlled the Aegean sea-coast from Thermopylae to the Propontis. His dominion on land extended from Thrace to Illyria, and included a substantial part of northern Greece.

Philip was a great commander, having reorganised the Macedonian army, and exploited its new weapon, a thirteen-foot spear as opposed to the usual six-foot spear of the Greek hoplites. In addition to a more powerful deployment of the phalanx, he also used cavalry with great skill. He was personally courageous and daring in battle, but also a considerable tactician. He was, too, a consummate diplomat and politician, knowing how to further his interests by making opportune alliances and friendships (including several marriages) and fostering pro-Macedonian factions within neighbouring powers. His early access to the gold of Thrace through control of Amphipolis increased his own resources and perhaps enabled him to use bribery as an instrument of policy. His court at Pella was home to visiting artists and intellectuals like Aristotle, who became the tutor of his son Alexander.

The Athenians were divided in their response to the rise of Macedonian power, There had long been a peace party that urged necessary accommodation with Philip. To some, his rise offered a positive opportunity. Isocrates saw in Philip the possible agent who could make his Panhellenic dream a reality, and in an open letter to him written after the peace in 346 urged Philip to lead the Greek states in a united campaign against Persia.

> When Athens held the principal power among the Greeks, and similarly when Sparta did, I do not think anything of the sort could have been attained, because each side could easily have frustrated the attempt. Now, however, I no longer take that view. All the states have, I know, been reduced by misfortune to one level, and I think they will be much more inclined to accept the benefits of unanimity than the old competitiveness.
>
> (*Philip*, 40)

The opposing view that Philip had to be stopped at all costs found a powerful advocate in the person of Demosthenes.

THE OPPOSITION OF DEMOSTHENES

Demosthenes' speeches to the Athenian assembly against Philip are among the most famous in the history of oratory. Indeed the title given to three of them, *Philippic*, has gone into general consciousness to mean a vigorous harangue. Though Philip is denounced, it is the Athenians who are harangued for their inactivity.

'Philip is dead' comes one report. 'No, he is only ill' from another. What difference does it make? Should anything happen to Philip, Athens, in her present frame of mind, will soon create another Philip. This one's rise was due less to his own power than to Athenian apathy.

(*Philippic*, I, 11)

The orator seeks to arouse his countrymen to the dangers of Philip's encroachment on Athenian and general Greek interests. In the speeches of Demosthenes, Philip emerges as an unscrupulous, restless, cunning and efficient figure, who will stop at nothing to increase his own power and thus threaten the liberties of all who come into contact with him. Each speech is a response to particular circumstances and includes practical suggestions for action. On more than one occasion, he urged the sending of a force to protect Athenian interests in northern Greece, not only consisting of mercenaries but made up with a substantial proportion of citizen soldiers, under citizen commanders and backed by naval support. He urged the Athenians to use the Theoric fund (designed for festival provision) for military purposes. Mercenaries were dispatched to Olynthus in 349/8, but Athens was distracted by the revolt of Euboea and they proved to be too few and too late.

A leading political figure at the time, Demosthenes was part of the embassy that negotiated peace with Philip in 346. Doubtless he regarded this as a necessary temporary expedient in the face of rebellious allies and diminishing resources. When Philip continued to interfere in Greek affairs even as far as the Peloponnese, he went on embassies to other states in an attempt to dissuade them from any Macedonian entanglement. He tried every means to bring the peace to an end. With their corn supplies threatened by Philip's activities in the Bosporus, the Athenians finally dispatched a flcct against him. Demosthenes endeavoured to organise a general Greek alliance; he was present at the battle of Chaeronea in 338. Philip's victory here was the beginning of the end of the independent Greek city states, which were now at the mercy of Philip, who might have marched against Athens if he had wished.

Demosthenes' speeches respond to the particular needs of their occasions but also contain recurring themes and a larger analysis. As a champion of liberty and democracy, he found all that Philip represented anathema. But he was not blind to the potential weaknesses of democratic government. On several occasions, he points out that assembly resolutions are value-less, unless there is the will to carry them out. Criticism of his fellow orators is a constant theme.

> I think the true citizen must put the reality of survival above the gratification of rhetoric. Since the appearance of our modern speakers, who ask 'What are your wishes? What proposal would you like? What can I do for your gratifi-cation?', Athenian strength has been squandered for immediate popularity.
>
> (*Olynthiac* III, 22)

The system of public scrutiny of officials in the military and civil areas of state might have an inhibiting and paralysing effect, as those holding executive office sought above all to avoid anything that might lead to investigation and prosecution. The very strengths of democracy could be weakening. Philip, who con-trolled the army, the state and the treasury, was answerable to no one and able to respond to any situation with efficiency, singlemindedness and speed. But more than this, Demosthenes believed that he was living in a period of national decline when the communal spirit and civic pride that had sustained Athens in the period of her greatness had been gravely undermined.

> Your predecessors had no flattery from speakers, and no love from them, as you do. But for forty-five years [between the Persian and the Peloponnesian Wars] they were the accepted leaders of the Greek states. They amassed over ten thousand talents on the Acropolis. The king of this district of Thrace was their subordinate, and stood in the right relation for a non-Greek to a Greek state. Many and great were the victories they won by land and sea as citizen fighters, and they were alone of mankind in leaving by their achievements a reputation high above carping envy. Such they proved in the sphere of Hellenic affairs. Look now at the character they bore in our city itself, in public and private relations alike. In the first the architectural beauty they created in sacred buildings and their adornment was of a quality and an extent unsurpassable by later generations. Their private lives were of such restraint, and so well in keeping with the

character of the community, that if the type of house lived in
by Aristides or Miltiades or any of the great men of that day
is known nowadays, it can be seen to be no grander than its
neighbours. No one then made capital out of public affairs.
It was felt that the community should be the gainer. But
their integrity in the conduct of Hellenic affairs, their
devotion in that of religion, their equity in that of private
concerns, gained them the highest happiness. So stood the
state in the past under the leaders I have mentioned. What is
the position now under our present splendid administrators?
Is there any similarity, any comparison with the past? I cut
short the long list of instances. You can all see the degree of
helplessness to which we have come. Sparta is finished.
Thebes is fully occupied. No other state is strong enough
to bid for the supremacy. We could retain our position in
safety and hold the scales of justice for the Hellenic world.
And yet we have lost territory of our own, we have spent
over fifteen hundred talents to no purpose, the allies we
made in the war have brought us down in the peace, and
we have brought an adversary of such magnitude on the
stage against us. I invite any man present to tell me here and
now, what other source there is of Philip's power than
ourselves. 'Well,' I am told, 'that may be very unfortunate,
but at home, at least, we are better off.' What is the evidence
of this? Plaster on the battlements, new streets, water
supplies. These are trivialities. Turn your eyes on the pur-
suers of these political ends. They have risen from beggary to
riches, from obscurity to prominence, and in some cases
have houses which outshine public buildings themselves,
while their consequence rises with the decline of the nation.

(Olynthiac III, 23)

If this analysis was correct, to reverse that national decline was
hardly within the power of one individual. Nevertheless, the
rhetorical appeal of Demosthenes rested upon the invocation
of former greatness.

The idea that Greece will be rescued by Chalcis or Megara,
while Athens eludes the issue, is wholly wrong. It will be
enough if these cities themselves survive. It is we who must
do it, we whose ancestors gained the glory and bequeathed
it in the course of great perils. And if each one of us is to

69

sit idle and press for his own requirements and his own exemption from duty, first of all he will never find anyone to do it for him, and secondly, I fear that all that we seek to avoid will be forced upon us.

(*Philippic* III, 75)

This is the note which he struck again in a famous self-defence, written in 330 after the policy had failed, against an old adversary, Aeschines, who had laid responsibility for the city's plight at Demosthenes' door.

If I presumed to say that it was I who inspired you with a spirit worthy of your past, there is not a man present who might not properly rebuke me. But my point is that these principles of conduct were your own, that this spirit existed in the city before me, and that in its particular application I had merely my share as your servant. Aeschines, however, denounces our policy as a whole, invokes your resentment against me as responsible for the city's terrors and risks, and in his anxiety to wrest from me the distinction of an hour, robs you of glories which will endure for ever. If you decide my policy was wrong, you will make it seem that your misfortunes are due, not to the unkindness of fortune, but to a mistake of your own. But it is not true, gentlemen, it is not true that you were mistaken when you took upon you that peril for the freedom and safety of Greece. No, by our fathers, who were first to face the danger at Marathon; by those who stood in the ranks at Plataea; by the fleets of Salamis and Artemisium; by all those many others who lie in the sepulchres of the nation, brave men whom Athens honoured and buried, all alike, Aeschines, not the successful only, nor only the victorious. She did well. They have all done what brave men may; their fate is that which God assigned.

(*On the Crown*, 199)

The conservative appeal of Demosthenes to the highest traditions of self-respecting freedom and political responsibility has been admired throughout the ages, though the wisdom of his policy has been questioned. Did he overestimate the spiritual and material resources of Athens, and exaggerate the malignancy of Philip, who seems to have sought understanding with

Athens, and in the event did not move against her in the hour of his victory?

ALEXANDER THE GREAT

In the year after Chaeronea, Philip called a conference of all the Greek states at Corinth and announced a decision to make war on Persia to liberate the Greek cities of Asia Minor and punish the Persians for acts of sacrilege committed in the days of Xerxes. Philip was to be the supreme commander of a Panhellenic force. On the eve of his setting sail, however, he was assassinated. He was succeeded by his young son Alexander, then aged 23, who was immediately faced with revolt on all fronts. He moved swiftly into Greece and had himself elected at Corinth as his father's successor as general of the Greeks. He had to quell rebellions first in Illyria and Thrace. When Thebes rebelled, he swiftly bore down upon the city and soon occupied it. It was razed to the ground (the only house left standing was that of the poet Pindar), and its inhabitants were sold into slavery. Like his father, he appreciated the achievements of Greek culture. It is reported that he carried with him on his campaigns an edition of Homer's *Iliad* prepared for him by his tutor Aristotle, and that at the supposed tomb of Achilles at Sigeum he pronounced the Greek hero fortunate in having such a herald of his fame. Having settled Greece, he immediately undertook the proposed expedition to Persia, and by the end of 334 he had liberated most of Asia Minor from Persian control. In 333 he defeated the Persian king Darius at the battle of the Issus. Having secured Phoenicia, Palestine and Egypt, he marched to Babylonia for the final reckoning with Darius, whom he brought to battle and defeated decisively at Gaugamela in 331. He then continued eastward beyond the Persian borders as far as north-west India and the Punjab, only stopping when his troops refused to go further. His conquests extended the Greek language and Greek institutions over the eastern world. At the same time, he envisaged a union between Greek and oriental, symbolised in his own marriage to Roxane and in his policy of encouraging intermarriage between the Macedonian élite and the conquered Persians. He also seems to have departed from Greek ways in taking over the *proskynesis*, or obeisance, traditionally reserved for the Persian kings. On his sudden death after twelve years of continuous conquest in 323, his empire was divided among his generals. In Greece, Athens and the northern states revolted against Macedonian rule but were defeated at the battle of Crannon in 322 by Antipater, who forced a new oligarchic constitution upon Athens and established a permanent Macedonian garrison. Athens had now lost both her freedom and her democracy.

The power struggle that followed Alexander's death produced three dynastic kingdoms stemming from his generals Antigonus, Seleucus and Ptolemy. The Antigonids controlled Macedonia and mainland Greece. They ruled from Macedonia but Athens remained a cultural centre. The Seleucids took over the old Persian empire with their capital at Antioch. The Ptolemies ruled Egypt and part of Asia Minor with their capital at Alexandria, which had been founded by Alexander on the Nile delta in 331. Its strategic position soon made it a great economic and industrial centre, and generous patronage by the Ptolemies, who set up its famous museum and library, made it a cultural capital as well. A cosmopolitan city of Egyptians, Greeks and Jews, by 200 it was the largest city in the world. In the late third century the Attalids established a fourth dynasty within Seleucid territory whose capital was Pergamum in north-west Asia Minor, a beautiful city famous for its school of sculpture and its library second only to that of Alexandria. Alexander's policy of colonisation began the Hellenisation of the east and Greek civilisation in a diluted form was diffused throughout the Hellenistic kingdoms.

In the late third century the growing power of Rome began to impinge upon the Greek world. By 133 all the old Hellenistic kingdoms had become part of the Roman empire. With the Roman conquest of Greece, Hellenism now spread westwards as the Greeks began to educate and civilise their uncultivated conquerors. As the Roman poet Horace (65–8) wrote in the Augustan age:

> Graecia capta ferum victorem cepit et artes
> Intulit agresti Latio
>
> Conquered Greece conquered her savage victor and brought the arts into rustic Latium

(Epistles II, 1, 156–7)

3

LITERATURE

The creation of poetry generally is due to two causes,
both rooted in human nature. The instinct for imitation is inherent in man from his earliest days. . . . Also
inborn in us is the instinct to enjoy works of imitation.
. . . The instinct for imitation, then, is natural to us, as
is also a feeling for music and for rhythm – and metres
are obviously detached sections of rhythms.

Aristotle, *Poetics*, IV

INTRODUCTION

For epic, Homer had used the dactylic hexameter, a line composed of six units or feet. Each unit (for which the Greek word is
metron, a measure) may be a dactyl, made up of a long syllable
followed by two short syllables (— ˘˘) or by a spondee, made up
to two long syllables (— —). Long and short refer to the time
taken in pronunciation, to the 'quantity' or length of the syllables. Greek metre, unlike English, is not determined by a pattern
of stressed and unstressed syllables. In literature after Homer, we
see the establishment of new material forms used for kinds that
developed after him. The elegaic couplet, consisting of a
hexameter followed by a pentameter, was used for epitaphs,
inscriptions and epigrams. It may be represented as follows:

— ˘˘ | — ˘˘ | — ˘˘ | — ˘˘ | — ˘˘ | — ˘˘

— ˘˘ | — ˘˘ | — | — ˘˘ | — ˘˘ | ˘

The pentameter line is actually two and a half feet repeated. The iambic, which later became the metre for the spoken parts of drama, was first used for occasional poems. The pattern of the iambic line is:

$$\cup \; \cup\cup \mid \cup \; \cup\cup \mid \cup \; \cup\cup \mid \cup \; \cup\cup \mid \cup \; \cup\cup \mid \cup \; \cup$$

At particular points in the line, the pattern allows syllables to be either long or short, thus making the metre very flexible. Both these forms were used by an early practitioner, Archilochus, of the mid-seventh century, fragments of whose work survive as the earliest post-Homeric poetry.

Early lyric poetry (called by the Greeks melic, whence melody, for it was always sung in public performance, often at a *symposium* or drinking party) has two main branches. The Aeolian, from Aeolia in northern Asia Minor, is monodic, that is composed for one voice, and monostrophic, that is written in stanzas that repeat the same metrical form. Its two main representatives, Sappho and Alcaeus of the late seventh century, both came from Lesbos and wrote in the Aeolic dialect of Greek. They have given their names to their favoured metrical forms, which they may have invented. Sappho seems to have been the centre of some kind of religious association, dedicated to Aphrodite and the Muses, which had young girls for its members. Much of her poetry is concerned with the lives and loves of these women. One of the most famous is quoted by the rhetorician Longinus in his treatise *On the Sublime*, cited here in the version of the eighteenth-century poet Ambrose Philips.

> Bless'd as the immortal gods is he,
> The youth who fondly sits by thee,
> And hears and sees thee all the while
> Softly speak and sweetly smile.
>
> 'Twas this deprived my soul of rest,
> And raised such tumults in my breast;
> For while I gazed, in transport tossed,
> My breath was gone, my voice was lost.
>
> My bosom glowed; the subtle flame
> Ran quick through all my vital frame;

O'er my dim eyes a darkness hung,
My ears with hollow murmurs rung.

In dewy damps my limbs were chilled,
My blood with gentle horrors thrilled;
My feeble pulse forgot to play,
I fainted, sunk, and died away.

Longinus then comments:

> Are you not astonished at the way in which, as though they
> were gone from her and belonged to another, she at one and
> the same time calls up soul and body, ears, tongue, eyes, and
> colour; how, uniting opposites, she freezes while she burns, is
> both out of her senses and in her right mind? For she is
> either terrified or not far from dying. And all this is done so
> that not one emotion may be seen in her, but a concourse of
> emotions. All such emotions as these are awakened in lovers,
> but it is, as I said, the selection of them in their most extreme
> forms and their fusion into a single whole that have given the
> poem its distinction.
>
> (10)

Another ancient critic, Dionysius of Halicarnassus, cites a poem
of Sappho to exemplify a polished style of composition where
there is metrical harmony, euphonious diction and a flowing
continuity (*On Literary Composition*, 23). Alcaeus wrote hymns to
the gods, war songs, political poems, love poems, encomia and
drinking songs. Only a little of the work of these early lyric poets
survives, mostly in the form of fragments. Many of these are
preserved on papyrus as illustrated in the fragment of Alcaeus
(fig. 10).

The Dorian choral lyric involving dancing developed at
Sparta and characteristically had a triadic structure involving
strophe, antistophe and epode (see p. 79). These grander choral
lyrics were invariably more public in character. There are many
kinds of choral lyric, e.g. the hymeneal, the hymn, the dithyramb
in honour of Dionysus, the threnody, the encomium. The
Theban poet Pindar (*c.* 518–*c.* 466), who used the Doric dialect
and form, wrote in all these kinds, but only his epinician or
triumphal odes celebrating the victories of competitors in the
Greek games (Olympian, Pythian, Isthmian and Nemean) survive in complete form, mostly having a triadic structure. His

75

Figure 10   A Greek papyrus

odes are heroic in tone, grandiloquent in expression and digressive in structure with mythical illustration; they celebrate aristocratic values. In his imitation of the second Olympian ode, the seventeenth-century poet Abraham Cowley, though, unlike Pindar or any other classical poet, he uses a verse form with a rhyme scheme, nevertheless manages to strike a note of grand enthusiasm reminiscent of Pindar's style and manner. The ode is in praise of the charioteer Theron, whose victory the poet associates with the mythical founder of the Olympian games, the heroic archetype Heracles (Alcides).

> Queen of all harmonious things,
>   Dancing words, and speaking strings,
>   What god, what hero wilt thou sing?
> What happy man to equal glories bring?
>   Begin, begin thy noble choice,
> And let the hills around reflect the image of thy voice.
>   Pisa does to Jove belong,
>   Jove and Pisa claim thy song.

The fair first-fruits of war, th'Olympic games,
    Alcides offered up to Jove;
    Alcides too thy strings may move;
But, oh, what man to join with these can worthy prove!
Join Theron boldly to their sacred names;
    Theron the next honour claims;
    Theron to no man gives place,
Is first in Pisa's, and in virtue's race;
    Theron there, and he alone,
Ev'n his own swift forefathers has outgone.

After a long mythological digression, the poet returns briefly to his subject, and in a celebrated passage allies his talent with the inexhaustible power of Nature figured in the soaring eagle of Zeus. Cowley is more diffuse than Pindar and hails the eagle as the bearer of Zeus' thunderbolts and for carrying off the beauteous youth Ganymede from earth to Olympus.

Let Art use method and good husbandry,
Art lives on Nature's alms, is weak and poor;
Nature herself has unexhausted store,
Wallows in wealth, and runs a turning maze,
    That no vulgar eye can trace.
    Art instead of mounting high,
About her humble food does hovering fly.
Like the ignoble crow, rapine and noise does love,
Whilst Nature, like the sacred bird of Jove,
Now bears loud thunder, and anon with silent joy
    The beauteous Phrygian boy,
Defeats the strong, o'ertakes the flying prey;
And sometimes basks in th'open flames of day.
    And sometimes too he shrouds,
    His soaring wings among the clouds.

TRAGEDY: FESTIVALS AND CONVENTIONS

Very little is known about the origins or even about the immediate antecedents of tragedy. The word itself means 'goat song' but the surviving plays have long lost any connection with rituals involving goats. Tragedy seems to have been an Athenian invention (little is recorded of drama in other cities) and was performed at the annual spring festival of the god Dionysus, called the Great or City Dionysia to distinguish it from the lesser rural festivities in honour of Dionysus. The Dionysia as a state institution is first associated with the tyrant Peisistratus and thereafter appears to have been reorganised by Cleisthenes. The city festival involving choral lyrics and drama was held over several days in March starting with a procession in honour of the god, for Peisistratus had established a temple on the south-eastern side of the Acropolis. The first dramas seem to have been acted in the Agora. A major advance is associated with the name of Thespis, the actor/dramatist (whence Thespian), who separated himself from the singing and dancing chorus to converse with the chorus leader. Aristotle accredits Aeschylus with the introduction of a second actor and Sophocles with a third (*Poetics*, IV). Comedies were introduced into the Dionysia shortly before the Persian Wars. By the time of the earliest extant play of Aeschylus, the city Dionysia consisted of a day of procession, followed by a contest in dithyrambic odes involving ten choruses, a day given over to comedies (five in number) and then three days of tragedies presented on a competitive basis. On each day, one playwright presented three tragic plays, which might be linked like the three plays that make up the Oresteian trilogy but usually were not related in plot (though it is difficult to believe that they did not form some sort of sequence in mood or theme). These were followed by something completely different, a grotesque satyr play, a kind of bawdy phallic romp, which doubtless had the function of providing comic relief at the end of the day. On the next and last day, judges (*kritai*, whence critic) drawn from the ten tribes and elected by lot gave their verdict. The competitive element existed from earliest times; Thespis is reputed to have won first prize for his drama in about 535. Plays might be revived in the rural Dionysia but had only one city performance. All our extant plays were written in the period after the Persian Wars and before the end of the Peloponnesian War. We have six plays by Aeschylus (525–456) and a record of more than eighty titles to his name. The authorship of the *Prometheus*, traditionally ascribed to him, has been disputed by some modern scholars. We have seven plays of Sophocles (*c.* 496–406), together with a record of 123 titles, and nineteen of Euripides (*c.* 485–406), together with a record of ninety-two titles. One satyr play by Euripides survives.

Arrangements for the festival were the responsibility of the eponymous archon (so called because his year of office was known and identified by his name), who chose from the wealthiest citizens a number of *choregoi*, who were required to pay for the training and equipping of a chorus. Some expenses were borne by the state. The archon also chose the playwrights (we do not know how); non-Athenians might and did apply and succeed. The role of a *choregos* was largely financial; the actual direction was left to the playwright, who not only wrote the play but also choreographed and provided the music. In the early days the playwright, like Thespis, was also an actor; with the addition of a second and third actor grew a class of professional actors, an honoured trade in Athens. In 449 prizes were instituted for actors. From the time of Pericles the state treasury paid for the seats of citizens, though non-citizens and foreigners were perhaps charged admission. Women may have been allowed to attend (there is some dispute about this) and even slaves, presumably if accompanying their masters.

Any modern visitor to the site of an ancient theatre (*theatron*, a watching place) will be impressed by its size. The so-called Periclean theatre of the 440s at Athens held about 14,000 spectators seated upon benches of wood, rising in tiers in a vast semicircle up the side of the Acropolis. This replaced the first theatre dating from the early fifth century. The stone theatre associated with the name of Lycurgus was completed in 330. The present theatre of Dionysus in Athens dates from Roman times. The vastness of the seating area, physical proof that ancient drama was community theatre, is complemented by the size of the performing area itself, dominated by a circle of about 60 feet in diameter in the centre of which was an altar to the god. The circle, called the *orchestra*, meaning dancing place, must have been largely the preserve of the chorus (ten in number in the plays of Aeschylus, fifteen in Sophocles and subsequently), who danced and sang to the accompaniment of flutes. (None of the dance movements or musical accompaniment survives.) The division of the choral odes into strophe (turn), antistrophe (counterturn) and epode (after song) probably reflects the movement of the chorus through the *orchestra*. The complicated choral metres may be related to particular steps. It is noticeable that in the *parodos*, the first utterance of the chorus as they enter the *orchestra*, the metre is often anapaestic ($\smile\smile - \smile\smile - \smile\smile -$, etc.), giving

Figure 11a   The theatre of Dionysus at Athens (*photograph: Richard Stoneman*)

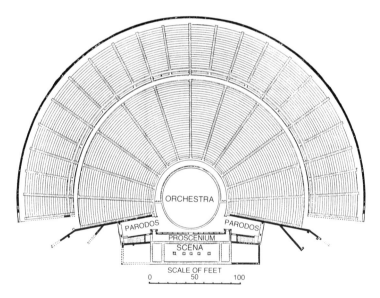

Figure 11b   The theatre at Epidauros

the rhythm of a march. It seems likely that a wooden stage beyond the *orchestra* was introduced at an early date, and in about 460 came the first background building (*skene*), perhaps containing dressing rooms for actors and an entrance on to the stage. This area must have been the preserve of the principal actors. When Clytemnestra tempts Agamemnon into the palace by way of the purple carpet in the opening play of the *Oresteia*, produced in 458, it is to be presumed that Agamemnon walks up steps on to a low stage – otherwise the carpet would not have been visible to the front rows of the audience – before entering the stage building. Nevertheless, all the acting took place out of doors in the open air. Any interior scenes might be played on the *ekkuklema*, probably a platform on wheels which could be rolled out, for example, in the *Oresteia* to reveal the bodies of Agamemnon and Cassandra killed off-stage by Clytemnestra (acts of violence were usually committed off-stage and reported). There was also a *mechane*, a crane by which a god might be lowered from the top of the theatre building, as for example in Euripides' *Electra* when Castor and Pollux descend to tidy up the loose ends of the plot. This use of the machine has given rise to the phrase 'deus ex machina' ('the god from the machine'). Gods also appeared on a balcony of the stage building called the *theologeion*.

The scale of the proceedings – the nearest spectators were a long way from the actors and the furthest were very distant indeed – precluded the development of naturalistic techniques in writing, staging or acting. Aristotle tells us that Sophocles introduced scene painting (*Poetics*, IV) but this can only have been very simple in effect; characters and chorus tell us in words where they are and what they are doing. As for acting, there must have been a particular style made necessary in large part by the physical conditions of the theatre. Even given the marvellous acoustics of the Greek theatre design, much effort must simply have been put into voice projection – Sophocles is said to have given up acting because he had a weak voice. Part of the acting style was dictated by conventional forms of attire. All performers (who were always male) wore masks and the principal actors also donned special high boots or buskins called *kothurnoi*. Nevertheless, individuality was allowed for in the painting of masks to represent particular characters, and they could be changed from scene to scene. After he had blinded himself off-stage at the end of the play to which he had given his name, King Oedipus doubtless entered with a blood-stained mask. Individuality could further be marked by the colourful costumes or by simple props, like a lyre for Apollo, a sceptre for a king or a broad-brimmed hat for a messenger. Effects were therefore simple and broad. In the intimate drama of today, much meaning is conveyed around the playwright's words by detailed and realistic setting, by significant small-scale gesture, by facial expression and even by the pregnant pause. But in the Greek theatre, nuance of gesture and effect would have been quite pointless, nor could the relation between player and audience be intimate. The chorus must have been trained in precise harmony and in beauty of movement when seen from afar; actors must have concentrated on conveying large effects and above all on giving a clear expressive rendering of the words themselves. And in composing those words, the playwright took for granted a need for clarity of emphasis in setting the scene, in announcing the entrances of characters and in making their emotional reactions fully explicit.

All plays consist of a number of episodes or scenes involving the principal characters, written in iambics (see p. 74), divided by choral interludes called *stasima*, written in a variety of metrical forms. In Aeschylus, the choral part amounts to a third of the play; in the third part of the *Oresteia*, the chorus of Furies, the Eumenides, who give their name to the play, are central to the action itself. Sophocles and Euripides reduced the proportional part of the chorus, though in particular plays it might still play a special role, as in the case of Euripides' *Bacchae*, where the chorus of Bacchanals bear witness to and define the nature and benefits of the Dionysiac experience. More commonly, the chorus is detached from the main actions involving the heroic figures of myth, but in comment and response is fully integrated into the emotional and thematic pattern of the play as a whole. The need to integrate the chorus with the main action and the comparative brevity of a Greek play when compared to a modern drama (approximately 1,500 lines in length including the chorus), determined by the festival production of four plays in one day, precluded the development of complicated plots involving more than one strand of action, variety of scenes (there is a scene change from Delphi to Athens in the *Eumenides* but this is rare) or complicated time sequences. Concentration of effect and a concern for unity of design are principles endemic in Greek art from Homer onwards. In drama simplicity and economy were further encouraged by limitations of time and form outside the playwright's control.

Greek drama was therefore a more stylised form than subsequent European drama, and the particular style was determined by inherited conventions connected with festival production and by the physical conditions of the theatre. But within the limitations imposed by the performance of the plays as part of a religious festival, what is striking is the remarkable freedom allowed to the individual dramatist, who is not restricted to myths involving Dionysus or subject to any kind of priestly control. Indeed, the earliest extant play, the *Persians* of Aeschylus (for which Pericles was *choregos*), is not mythological at all, but takes its subject from recent history. The only sense in which the playwright is a priest is figurative: he is a priest of the Muses. And if Greek drama developed from some form of religious ritual, then it quickly freed itself from the restrictions implied in the word ritual, which is not appropriately used to describe Greek tragedy.

AESCHYLUS (525–456)

Tragedy is a phenomenon that came into existence simultaneously with the gradual transformation of the Athenian state into a democracy. Though Thespis dates from the latter days of the tyranny of Peisistratus, that tyranny itself, comparatively enlightened in character, marked a stage in the destruction of the archaic aristocratic order, whose power was formally extinguished with the reform of the Areopagus in 462–461. Our oldest extant tragedy concerns an event without which that transformation would not have been possible, the triumph of Greece in the Persian Wars. What makes the play more than a national and patriotic celebration of the heroic freedom fighters of Marathon and Salamis (Aeschylus himself had fought at Marathon) is that events are set entirely in Persia and no individual Greek is named. A chorus of Persian elders and Atossa, the mother of Xerxes, are anxious about the fate of the expedition. Atossa makes libations before the tomb of her dead husband Darius, whose ghost then appears and when informed of the disaster castigates Xerxes for rashness and folly, particularly remarking his impiety in seeking to fetter the

Hellespont and in burning the temples of the Greeks. Old oracles are being fulfilled through the behaviour of his son: 'when man makes haste the god assists' (1. 742): human folly accelerates the fulfilment of the gods' plans. Darius also sees divine justice in the fate of the Persians.

> they wait; and there wait too
> Ruin and untold pain, which they must yet endure –
> The just reward of pride and godless insolence.
> Marching through Hellas, without scruple they destroyed
> Statues of gods, burned temples; levelled with the ground
> Altars and holy precincts, now one heap of rubble.
> Therefore their sacrilege is matched in suffering.
> And more will follow; for the well-spring of their pain
> Is not yet dry; soon new disaster gushes forth.
> On the Plataean plain the Dorian lance shall pour
> Blood in unmeasured sacrifice; dead heaped on dead
> Shall bear dumb witness to three generations hence
> That man is mortal, and must learn to curb his pride.
> For pride will blossom; soon its ripening kernal is
> Infatuation; and its bitter harvest, tears.
>
> (ll. 806–20)

Xerxes then returns; the fallen prince, now dressed in rags, laments the fate of the slain. Historically, Darius had been as ambitious as Xerxes, but Aeschylus with a poet's licence idealises him so that he appears as a wise old king. The downfall of the Persian enterprise results more from the envy of the gods than from the prowess of the Greeks. *Hybris*, bringing in its wake *ate* (infatuation or folly), begets its inevitable *nemesis*. But the pride and fall are not represented complacently. Aeschylus humanises the Persians to the extent that we are moved to reflect upon the perilous insecurity of any mighty endeavour and upon the radical instability of human fortune. It may be useful to reflect that it is unthinkable that any Elizabethan playwright could have dramatised the defeat of the Spanish Armada in such a way so soon after it had happened.

All the other surviving tragedies feature the heroic figures of traditional myths. Since these are many and multiform, they offer almost limitless potential for individual treatment. The Orestes myth used by Aeschylus in the one surviving trilogy, the *Oresteia*, is a case in point, being used in quite different ways by Homer, Aeschylus, Sophocles and Euripides.

The story of Orestes features almost as a recurrent leitmotif in counterpoint to the main theme in Homer's *Odyssey*. There Agamemnon returns from Troy to be met by his cousin Aegisthus, the son of Thyestes, who takes him back to his palace where he feasts and then kills him (IV, 521–37). What Agamemnon did not know was that Aegisthus had earlier prevailed upon his wife Clytemnestra to become her paramour, thus usurping Agamemnon's bed and throne (III, 254–75). The spirit of Agamemnon tells Odysseus that Clytemnestra murdered Cassandra; he regards Aegisthus as the principal agent in the plot against himself (XI, 405–34). The usurpers reigned for seven years until Orestes, as the gods foretold, returned to avenge his father by slaying Aegisthus. 'When Orestes had done the deed, he invited his friends to a banquet for the mother he loathed and the craven Aegisthus' (III, 303–10). Homer does not directly say how Clytemnestra died. Much is made of her infidelity, which the spirit of Agamemnon contrasts with the virtue of the loyal Penelope (XXIV, 192–202). The vengeance of Orestes is hailed as a glorious act not only by mortals such as Nestor and Telemachus but also by Zeus (I, 30) and Athene, who holds up the bravery of Agamemnon's son as an example to the son of Odysseus (I, 298–301). Divine approval for Orestes reflects divine support for the suitor-slaying which is the prelude of the re-establishment of order in the house of Odysseus. Aegisthus and the suitors die through their own wickedness and folly. Poetic justice is unequivocally upheld in either case.

The *Agamemnon* of Aeschylus opens with the night watchman at dawn on the roof of the king's palace catching sight of the beacon that announces the downfall of Troy. The chorus of Argive elders then set the emotional, thematic and mythological scene by recalling the setting out of the expedition led by Agamemnon, dwelling upon an event not mentioned by Homer. At Aulis the fleet had been marooned by contrary winds. A priest tells Agamemnon that the anger of the goddess Artemis will be appeased only by the sacrifice of his daughter Iphigeneia. Agamemnon is faced with a choice: he can return home in failure and risk the censure of men, or he can persevere with the great expedition (whose aim is supported by Zeus) after the crime of sacrifice. The first course is unthinkable: 'he puts on the yoke of necessity' (l. 217). The priest had predicted inevitable atonement for the slaughter of a child, and the chorus now fear its fulfilment: as the Libation-bearers put it, 'the guilty doer must suffer' (*drasanti pathein*, l. 313). The chorus introduce another great theme that will be worked out through the human action. In the midst of their song they invoke Zeus 'whoever he is' (l. 160), he who had overthrown Cronos and the old order and he who has ordained that through suffering comes knowledge or wisdom '*pathei mathos*' (l. 177). At the end of their song it is Justice who inclines the scales to exact wisdom at the price of suffering (l. 250). The stage is now set for the fulfilment of the priest's words. Clytemnestra, with the heart and soul of a man (l. 351), takes the leading role. She welcomes Agamemnon and masters him psychologically, exposing his weakness in the carpet scene. As she follows him into the palace, she prays to Zeus, the fulfiller (l. 973). The actual murder she accomplishes by throwing a net over him as he bathes and then stabbing him repeatedly. Aegisthus, insultingly called 'woman' by the chorus (l. 1625), pronounces Agamemnon's death a just requital for the iniquity of his father Atreus, who in a dispute with his brother Thyestes had served up his sons (Aegisthus' brothers) in a 'Thyestean' feast.

In the *Libation Bearers*, Orestes returns to execute the orders of Apollo in avenging this father. He kills Aegisthus first, then confronts Clytemnestra with her crime. As she pleads with him he hesitates, asking the hitherto silent Pylades if he should spare her. 'Where then are Apollo's words?' (l. 900) answers Pylades. For the crime of matricide, Orestes incurs the persecution of the Furies (not mentioned in Homer) who avenge crimes committed between kin.

In the *Eumenides* Orestes has sought sanctuary and the protection of Apollo, who ordered his crime at Delphi. While the Furies sleep, Apollo directs him to go to Athens to seek justice from Athene. The spirit of Clytemnestra awakes the Furies and goads them to hunt Orestes to his death. The Furies rebuke Apollo for interference. 'What about crimes by a wife against her husband?' he asks. They are not blood kin, the Furies reply (l. 212). Athene, having heard the pleas of Orestes and the Furies, decides to submit the case to a tribunal of twelve Athenian judges in her temple on the hill of Ares. The court she estab-

lishes is to endure for all time (ll. 482 ff.). Apollo appears as a
witness on Orestes' behalf. Athene gives her verdict in favour of
Orestes when the votes cast are equal. Much of the argument
has been over the primacy of male or female. Though female,
Athene was not born of woman, having sprung from the head of
Zeus. On this basis she gives her support to the male principle.
She then proceeds to placate the Furies, who as an order of gods
older than the Olympians (Zeus had come to power by replacing
Cronos, as the chorus in the *Agamemnon* had reminded us) feel
that the younger gods have overridden ancient laws. Athene
gives a second reason: Zeus through the oracle had given
witness that Orestes should not suffer for his deed. Athene
promises the Furies honour and abode in Athens. They, now
transformed into the Kindly Ones, yield to her persuasion,
which Athene identifies with Zeus (l. 974).

Aeschylus' interest in and presentation of the myth are therefore very different from those of Homer, who for his purposes
had stressed the infidelity of Clytemnestra, the wrong done to
Agamemnon and Orestes' just revenge which met with the gods'
approval. In the *Oresteia*, the myth serves as a vehicle for the
dramatic expression of a conflict between men and women
involved in a blood feud and between the rival claims of
different generations of gods. The conflict has both a political
and a religious dimension which are not easily separable. The
victory of the Olympian gods of the upper world, Apollo and
Athene, together with the mitigation of the older Furies (deities
from the nether world) which is attributed to the unseen workings of Zeus through persuasion, has clear symbolic force. 'Cry
sorrow, sorrow,' sings the chorus (*Agamemnon*, l. 121) 'but may the
good prevail.' The good that prevails after all the individual
suffering is a communal good, the establishment of Athenian
justice sanctioned by the gods. The learning that comes through
suffering in the *Oresteia* docs not, therefore, come by way of the
individual soul but comes by divine dispensation from without.
The court scene on the Areopagus is clearly designed to represent what was historically the solution to the old tribal system of
justice through bloodfeud in the development of the laws and
institutions of the *polis*. The resolution of the conflict in historic
terms, and the celebration of Athens at the close, mean that the
drama in its overall effect is not, in the fullest sense of the word,
tragic. In the greatest tragedy we are caught up in the fate of

individual protagonists and are not to be deflected by the compensation of ameliorating social or political consequences. But for all that, the *Oresteia* is not a comfortable experience. In the court scene, we may feel that in their bizarre arguments the gods work in mysterious ways that reflect the arbitrariness with which judgements are frequently arrived at in human courts of justice. Furthermore, although the play offers an escape from the cycle of crime and guilt and countercrime, it also puts us into raw contact with the primitive roots of human behaviour which the social institutions of civilisation are designed to restrain. Although the protagonists become entangled in a fatal net that is not of their own devising, they also show a determined will- ingness for ruthless action and a capacity for unholy deeds that is appalling, the effect of which is most feelingly dramatised in the prophecies and fate of the innocent Cassandra before she is murdered alongside Agamemnon. The burden of what has gone before is by no means lifted or transmuted by the end.

SOPHOCLES (*c.* 496–406)

The note of celebration apparent in the *Oresteia* is also to be found in a famous choral ode in Sophocles' *Antigone*:

Wonders are many on earth, and the greatest of these
Is man, who rides the ocean and takes his way
Through the deeps, through wind-swept valleys of perilous
    seas
    That surge and sway.

He is master of ageless Earth, to his own will bending
The immortal mother of gods by the sweat of his brow,
As year succeeds to year, with toil unending
    Of mule and plough.

He is lord of all things living; birds of the air,
Beasts of the field, all creatures of sea and land
He taketh, cunning to capture and ensnare
    With sleight of hand;

Hunting the savage beast from the upland rocks,
Taming the mountain monarch in his lair,
Teaching the wild horse and the roaming ox
    His yoke to bear.

The use of language, the wind-swift motion of brain
He learnt; he found out the laws of living together
In cities, building him shelter against the rain
    And wintry weather

There is nothing beyond his power. His subtlety
Meeteth all chance, all danger conquereth.
For every ill he hath found its remedy,
    Save only death.

O wondrous subtlety of man, that draws
To good or evil ways! Great honour is given
And power to him who upholdeth his country's laws
    And the justice of heaven.

But he that, too rashly daring, walks in sin
In solitary pride to his life's end,
At door of mine shall never enter in
    To call me friend.

                          (329–70)

But the celebration is not wholly unequivocal. The Greek word translated 'wonder', *deinos*, has a range of meanings including terrible, clever and marvellous, and, at the end of the ode, it is clear that the chorus believe that the power of contrivance which is the subject of the song can lead to evil as well as to good. The song is prompted by the news that the edict of King Creon (that the body of Polyneices, the son of Oedipus, be not buried), has been flouted. Polyneices with his Argive allies had stormed the gates of Thebes and been killed in battle by his twin brother Eteocles. Creon, who at the beginning of the play has inherited the throne of Thebes, decrees the penalty of death for anyone burying Polyneices, whom he regards as an enemy of the city. At this point the chorus do not know what the audience already knows, that Antigone, the sister of Polynciccs, has donc the deed. The distinction they make at the end of their song between the man who is *hypsipolis*, high in state, in revering justice and the laws of the land (*nomous chthonos*) and the cityless outcast, the *apolis*, who does wrong for the sake of daring may seem at first to suggest Creon and Antigone respectively. Creon has already asserted that he is acting on behalf of the highest interests of the city whose laws he is protecting (ll. 184–95). But Antigone, who feels compelled to honour the rights of her kin, in confessing the deed to Creon, invokes justice that dwells with the gods below (chthonic powers) and draws a distinction between human proclamations and the unwritten and unfailing ordinances of the gods that are age-old and everlasting (ll. 450–7). Sophocles might therefore be said to have constructed his tragedy upon the conflicting claims of family and city represented in two individuals of strong and uncompromising will. There is no movement towards the resolution of the conflicting claims as in the *Oresteia* of Aeschylus, nor do the gods intervene to mark a way forward. Creon becomes more tyrannical, condemning Antigone to be immured in a cave. He refuses to heed the pleas of his son Haemon, who is betrothed to Antigone. After a fierce confrontation with the prophet Tiresias, who tells him that the gods are affronted by the unburied corpse, he finally relents, fearing the force of established laws (l. 1114), and sets out to free Antigone only to find Haemon clasping her dead body, for she has committed suicide. Haemon thrusts at Creon with his sword, but misses and then kills himself. Creon returns to the palace to find that his wife Eurydice has hanged herself in despair. No longer, if ever, the man who is *hypsipolis*, at the end, Creon recognises that his fate has reduced him to less than nothing.

Antigone, probably written in the 440s, is one of the three surviving plays, written at different periods, featuring members of the house of Oedipus, often printed together and given the title *The Theban Plays*. Not only were they not a trilogy in themselves, but the individual plays were not parts of other trilogies. Aristotle seems to have had *King Oedipus* (c. 429) particularly in mind when he gave his famous account of 'the best sort' of tragedy in his *Poetics*. Much of what he has to say is by way of comment on the plot.

King Oedipus certainly embodies the classical ideal of the well-made play. Everything follows on logically and naturally from the plague, which sets the plot in motion. That is not to say that it is a naturalistic play. That the palace servant who saved the infant Oedipus by giving him to a Corinthian servant should also have been the witness to the murder of Laius and that the same Corinthian servant should also be the bearer of the news of the death of Polybus are coincidences that might stretch the imagination if we were forced to reflect upon them. The legend or story of Oedipus is full of absurdities that are concealed or disguised by a Sophoclean sleight of hand in the plotting of the play. When the prophet Tiresias in anger tells Oedipus that the killer of his father Laius is present and will be found to be the son and husband to the mother who bore him (ll. 447–60) we do not know at this stage that Oedipus has been given an oracle that he will kill his father and marry his mother. Such knowledge at this point would have made the scene incredible. We only learn of the king's knowledge of this oracle much later in the play, when he tells Jocasta of his reasons for leaving his supposed parents Polybus and Merope in Corinth. Here it may be noted that Oedipus did not suffer from the complex to which he has given his name since he did all in his power to remove himself from his supposed parents.

The interweaving of the three oracles in the play (all truly Delphic in being difficult to interpret and only partial truths) is most skilfully done. That Jocasta should seek to deny the validity of oracles by telling another oracle (true, unbeknown to her) that Laius would die by the hand of his own child, because she supposes that the child of Laius has been exposed at birth and because it is believed in Thebes that Laius had been killed by robbers (in the plural), is one of the many powerful ironies of the plot.

The denouement is singled out for praise by Aristotle in a notable passage in the *Poetics*:

> Some plots are simple and some complex. . . . A complex action is one in which the change [of fortune] is accompanied by a discovery (*anagnoresis*) or a reversal (*peripeteia*), or both. These should develop out of the very structure of the plot . . . a reversal is a change from one state of affairs to its opposite, one which conforms, as I have said, to probability or necessity. In *Oedipus*, for example, the Messenger who came to cheer Oedipus and relieve him of his fear about his mother did the very opposite by revealing to him who he was . . . a discovery is a change from ignorance to knowledge. . . . The most effective form of discovery is that which is accompanied by reversals like the one in *Oedipus* . . . a discovery of this kind in combination with a reversal will carry with it either pity or fear.
>
> (X, XI)

The Corinthian messenger comes to give Oedipus news that Polybus is dead and that the Corinthians may make him king

91

of all the isthmus (ll. 939–41). In this news both Jocasta and Oedipus see the defeat of the oracles but, when Oedipus is still fearful that his mother is still alive, the messenger reveals that he had received the infant Oedipus from a shepherd in Laius' household. Jocasta sees the truth and begs Oedipus to desist but ironically he misinterprets her motives, thinking she fears that he may be low-born. He hails himself the child of chance (l. 1080). The chorus joyfully speculate that he is the son of a god. Then the servant of Laius is called and the truth is revealed, so that the reversal and discovery are completed.

The audience of course has known the truth all along, as the myth existed long before Sophocles and is known to Homer, for Odysseus encounters Jocasta, whom he calls Epicaste, in the underworld. When, therefore, Oedipus says at the opening of the play, 'I am here to learn for myself, I Oedipus, whose name is known from far', he is thinking of the fame he has acquired through his intelligence in solving the riddle of the Sphinx, whereas his real fame, before and after Freud, has always stemmed from parricide and mother-marrying. So much that he says has a double significance. No other Greek play (perhaps no other play at all) has exploited this dramatic irony so ruth-lessly, and much of the play's impact and symbolic force lie in the ignorance and blindness of Oedipus brought out in the play's plot, its imagery and its language, in the contrast between the blind prophet Tiresias who knows and the seeing Oedipus who does not know, and in the reversal when the knowing Oedipus blinds himself because he cannot bear to look upon the light of day. (In Homer there is no mention of the self-blinding: Oedipus lives on in Thebes haunted by the Furies of his mother, *Odyssey* XI, 271–80.)

The play therefore seems to fulfil Aristotelian requirements for a tragic fall:

> We saw that the structure of tragedy at its best should be complex, not simple, and that it should represent actions capable of awakening fear and pity. . . . It follows in the first place that good men should not be shown passing from prosperity to misery, for this does not inspire pity, it merely disgusts us. Nor should evil men be shown progressing from misery to prosperity. This is the most untragic of all plots, for it has none of the requisites of tragedy; it does not appeal to

our humanity, or awaken pity or fear in us. Nor again should an utterly worthless man be seen falling from prosperity into misery. Such a course might indeed play upon our humane feelings, but it would not arouse either pity or fear; for our pity is awakened by undeserved misfortune and our fear by that of someone just like ourselves. . . . There remains a mean between these extremes. This is the sort of man who is not conspicuous for virtue and justice and whose fall into misery is not due to vice and depravity, but rather to some error (*hamartia*), a man who enjoys prosperity and a high reputation like Oedipus.

(Poetics, XIII)

Although Aristotle begins with the best structure (he calls plot 'the soul of tragedy': character comes second: *Poetics*, VI) he imperceptibly moves into the question of character, though it should be noted that he never uses the term 'tragic hero'. As to the character of Oedipus, it is clear that he has faults; he is quick to anger and, though the killing of Laius (as narrated at ll. 798–813) may be regarded as a justifiable homicide in self-defence after provocation, his rash temper is apparent in his treatment of Creon and Tiresias. But despite the choral utterance 'pride (*hybris*) breeds the tyrant' (l. 872), Oedipus, unlike Xerxes in the *Persians*, in no sense merits his fall, for he did all in his power to avoid his predicted fate. He is not the victim of a 'tragic flaw' within himself – indeed the famous term *hamartia* is not now generally interpreted to mean more than error. Whatever his faults, Sophocles has endowed Oedipus with great qualities. A contrast might be made here with his counterpart in the *Oedipus* of the Roman playwright Seneca (4 BC–AD 65). He is a commanding presence who exhibits a concern for his people at the beginning and the end of the play; he is strong, assertive and single-minded in his quest for the truth, though Tiresias, Jocasta and the shepherd all try to deflect him: 'I will know who I am' (l. 1085). Above all, the responsibility he takes upon himself throughout is not relinquished after the terrible revelation. Of the blinding, he asserts: 'Apollo has laid this terrible agony upon me; not by his hand, I did it' (ll. 1329–31). The horror he feels in his unspeakable suffering is that of a civilised sensitivity and in the turmoil of his reactions he is able to think beyond himself to the future of his children, and to determine his own banishment.

The final words spoken to him by Creon 'Command no more.
Obey. Your rule is ended' (l. 1522) highlight the utter change of
fortune but are addressed to a noble spirit that is not utterly
broken.

If we take Aristotle's definition of tragedy:

> Tragedy then is a representation (*mimesis*) of an action that is
> worth serious attention, complete in itself, and of some
> amplitude . . . presented in the form of action not narra-
> tion; by means of pity and fear bringing about the purgation
> (*katharsis*) of such emotions.
>
> (*Poetics*, VI)

then the actions of Oedipus in the play, which are all freely
entered into, dramatise not merely the terrible insecurity of
human happiness (the moral of the chorus at the end) but a
hopeless human struggle against an inscrutable fate. Yet though
the chorus see in the fate of Oedipus the lesson that life is
nothing, in our experience of the play, man emerges as more
than 'the vile worm' that he is for the Psalmist in the Old
Testament. Our response to Oedipus does indeed include pity
and fear, but amongst other emotions is surely an element of
admiration for his greatness of spirit. How precisely this emotional effect might be cathartic (indeed what the meaning of the
word *katharsis* is) it is difficult to say. It seems that Aristotle's
theory was designed to ascribe to tragedy a positive and wholesome emotional function and to reinstate it as the central genre
against the moral objections of Plato, who had excluded all
poetry but encomia of famous men and hymns to the gods
from his ideal republic.

EURIPIDES (c. 485–406)

The earliest surviving play by Euripides, the latest of the three
tragedians, is his *Medea* of 431. The nurse acting as prologue
recalls how Medea out of love for Jason had helped him gain the
Golden Fleece and had been involved in the murder of his uncle
Pelias, as a result of which they had fled with their children to
settle in Corinth. But Jason has betrayed Medea for a marriage
to Glauce, daughter of Creon the king of Corinth. Medea
bitterly records the solemn oaths given to her by Jason.
Euripides then has her speak of her plight in such a way as to

show great sympathy with the actual social position of women in the Greek society of his times, and the powerlessness of foreign women in particular:

> Surely of all creatures that have life and will, we women
> Are the most wretched. When, for an extravagant sum,
> We have bought a husband, we must then accept him as
> Possessor of our body. This is to aggravate
> Wrong with worse wrong. Then the great question: will the
>   man
> We get be bad or good? For women, divorce is not
> Respectable; to repel the man, not possible.
> . . . If a man grows tired
> Of the company at home, he can go out, and find
> A cure for tediousness. We wives are forced to look
> To one man only.
>
> (ll. 230–51)

In Aristophanes' comedy *The Poet and the Women*, Euripides is tried by a court of women on the charge of misogyny; like other comic shafts against him, this barb has stuck. But a true misogynist would not have represented Medea sympathetically as Euripides does at the beginning of the play. The chorus of Corinthian women agree that her desire for revenge upon Jason is just. Creon then enters and orders Medea to take her sons into exile; in spite of his fear of her, he grants her request that sentence be delayed for a day. In a remarkable ode, the chorus see a great reversal of roles: it is men who break oaths; women's reputation for faithlessness will be ended. If Apollo had granted his gifts to women, they would counter the misogyny of men, for time records good and bad of men and women alike (ll. 410–30).

In the ensuing confrontation between husband and wife the egotistical Jason cuts a sorry figure. If only she had accepted things and kept quiet, she need not have been banished. To Medea's recriminations, he recognises that he needs all his powers of speech. Euripides has been criticised for making his characters indulge in clever talking or sophistry. He certainly has a particular fondness for the cut and thrust of line-by-line debate, *stichomythia* (which is present in all the dramatists). If Jason talks like a sophist here, then his sophistry has dramatic point. He says that she did what she did for him through *eros*, though he recognises a debt. Nevertheless, he, the oath-breaker, claims in bringing her, a foreigner, to Greece to have given her the benefits of Greek life under the rule of law, where she is now famous. Moreover, the marriage will bring prosperity and security not just for him but for her children. The chorus admire his prowess with words but tell him to his face that he was wrong to betray his wife. Given his character in Euripides, Jason's ultimate misogyny and xenophobia (ll. 1323–50) can scarcely be imagined to be the main burden of the play's meaning.

Having gained asylum from the visiting Athenian Aegeus, who also deplores Jason's conduct, she reveals her terrible plan for revenge. She will send her children to Glauce with a gift of a poisonous dress in which she will expire in agony. Then she will kill her sons. She prefers guilt to the mockery of her enemies (l. 797). The chorus try to dissuade her and, in a famous ode in praise of Athens, ask how the city of wisdom and beauty can give asylum to one who has murdered her children (ll. 824–50).

The climax of the play is a long monologue in which Medea wavers over her intention to kill her children (ll. 1020–80): 'Oh, what am I to do?' – in Aeschylus, Orestes had asked the same question of Pylades, who had invoked the command of Apollo. Here, although Medea is in the presence of the chorus, she is really addressing herself, her own *thymos*, her own heart or spirit, and there is no interplay between the human and the divine. The action of the play is entirely determined by the human agents. In a long self-analysis which reflects the agony of her divided soul and the various emotional shifts that have brought her to this pass, her maternal feelings struggle against her desire for revenge against Jason (in particular her desire not to be a laughing stock). Although she recognises that her sons will be doomed anyway as they will be killed for their part in the murder of Glauce, she is fully conscious of the wickedness of her action:

> I learn what evils I am about to do
> But passion (*thymos*) overmasters sober thought
> And this is the course of direst ills to human beings
> (ll. 1078–80)

We may compare here the words of Phaedra as she contemplates the love that she feels for her stepson Hippolytus:

We know the good; we apprehend it clearly,
But we can't bring it to achievement
(ll. 380–1)

Medea's words amount to a chillingly calm expression of clear self-knowledge. She is alarmingly rational, knows what she is doing and passes judgement on herself.

In making Medea pronounce so consciously upon her own wrongdoing it has been suggested that Euripides had in mind the Socratic doctrine that wrongdoing results from a faulty perception of the good, that virtue is knowledge and that 'no one willingly does wrong'. The Greek word in the Socratic formulation *hamartanei* brings to mind the word *hamartia*, or error, made famous by Aristotle in his *Poetics*. Oedipus makes his error unconsciously and unwillingly, though with apparent freedom of the will; Medea makes hers consciously and with similar freedom of the will, nor does she repent of it as she confronts the hapless and helpless Jason in bitter triumph at the end of the play in a chariot drawn by dragons above the stage. Certainly Euripides' representation of actual human nature is radically different from the ideal of it made famous by the Platonic Socrates, stressing as it does the intractable power of irrational forces in human affairs, which are manifested here in the extremity of Medea's revenge (and intensified by Euripides, for the motif of infanticide is believed to be his own addition to the myth). At the same time, the rationalist poet and liberal humanist of Periclean Athens seeks understanding of the cause of that irrationality and takes great pains to make Medea's motives sympathetically comprehensible.

Aristotle records the remark of Sophocles that while he portrays men as they ought to be (of the heroic stature of Oepidus or Antigone), Euripides portrays them as they are (*Poetics*, XXV). This contrast is most apparent in their different treatments of the myth of Orestes, which is not made the occasion for heroic action in Euripides' *Electra* as it is in the Sophoclean drama of the same name. The democratic note is clear in Euripides from the beginning. Electra has been forced into a marriage with a peasant on whose farm the action is set. He treats her with respectful kindness and has not forced consummation of the marriage. When told about him, Orestes reflects that true nobility has little to do with noble birth: all men including the well-born must be judged by their relationships (ll. 367–90). While characters are strong in Sophocles, in Euripides they are subject to weakness and fear. The Sophoclean Electra is a figure whom suffering has made resolute and single-minded; in Euripides she breaks down at the end. His Clytemnestra is not the proud, unrelenting character of Sophocles but a pitiable figure admitting to frailty and expressing regret for the revenge she took against Agamemnon. His Orestes questions the wisdom of the oracle and is goaded into action by Electra's accusation of weakness. After the matricide the chorus rebuke her for persuading him against his will. The Sophoclean Orestes has unquestioning faith and does not hesitate. In Aeschylus, Orestes is appalled and hesitates but no one doubts the reality of the threat of divine vengeance if he fails to act. Where Sophocles plays down the effect of matricide by making no mention of retribution in the form of Furies for Orestes and by making the climax of his play the killing of Aegisthus, thus ending upon a note of uncomplicated rejoicing at the cleansing of the house, the overthrow of tyranny and the assertion of justice, Euripides, having disposed of Aegisthus first (he is stabbed in the back while performing a sacrifice), makes the climax of his play the horror and torment felt by both daughter and son at the murder of their mother.

The resolution of the play is effected by the sudden appearance of the gods from the machine, Castor and Pollux, who pronounce Clytemnestra's fate just but do not justify Orestes and Electra, saying that Apollo's command was not wise. This critical spirit is in marked contrast to Sophocles. Electra is to marry Pylades, Orestes must stand trial in Argos. He will be acquitted on equal votes 'And this shall stand as precedent for murder trials in times to come that the accused when votes are equal win the case' (ll. 1265–9). How different is this almost gratuitous aetiology from the complicated Aeschylean resolution that had grown out of the evolving conflict of wills on both the human and divine planes. Euripides' gods are here merely machines for tying up the loose ends of the plot. In other plays (notably the *Hippolytus* and the *Bacchae*) gods representing non-rational forces are fully integrated into the thematic structure.

As if to emphasise the sceptical spirit in which the poet handles traditional stories, the gods announce that Clytemnestra is to be buried by Helen (her sister) and Menelaus, who are just now returning from Egypt, for 'Zeus sent off to Troy a phantom Helen to stir up strife and slaughter in the human race' (ll. 1282–3). We may recall here an earlier ode in which the chorus told how Pan brought a lamb with a golden fleece to Atreus' house, and how his brother Thyestes lay with Atreus' wife and took the lamb to his own house, whereupon Zeus in anger reversed the course of the stars and the sun's chariot. Such is the story, they say, but they do not believe that Zeus turned back the sun for any mortal misdeed. But such frightening tales (*mythoi*) are useful to mortals, as they promote reverence for the gods (ll. 699–746). And so the chorus scrutinise the myths; the characters and the gods from the machine question Apollo's oracle. Old certainties are not taken for granted in Euripides.

There is evidence that, of all the tragic poets, Euripides was held in the greatest regard. Plutarch (AD *c.* 50–*c.*120) relates the following remarkable anecdote about the fate of Athenians captured in Sicily:

> There is a tradition that many of the Athenian soldiers who returned home safely visited Euripides to thank him for their deliverance which they owed to his poetry. Some of them told him that they had been given their freedom in return for teaching their masters all they could remember of his works, while others, when they took flight after the final battle, had been given food and water for reciting some of his lyrics.
>
> (*Life of Nicias*, 29)

OLD COMEDY: ARISTOPHANES (*c.* 450–*c.* 385)

The origins of comedy were obscure to Aristotle but he records the view that the word is derived from *kome*, a village, because comedians were turned out of towns and went strolling around the villages (*Poetics*, III), rather than *komos*, revel, the preferred derivation of modern scholars. Revels which took place on festival days might end with the participants parading the streets, garlanded and with torches, singing, dancing, drinking and making merry. Aristotle also says that comedy came from improvisations connected with phallic songs (associated with fertility and the worship of Dionysus) still surviving in the

LITERATURE

institutions of many of the cities of his day, and that the earliest
plot makers were Sicilian.

In Athens comedy, like tragedy, was a state institution performed at the Great Dionysia and also at a special festival in
January called the Lenaia. The chorus (consisting of twenty-four
members who might be divided into two half-choruses) was
provided by a *choregos* whose responsibility it was to hire, train
and fit out its members at his own expense. The actors, whose
number does not seem to have been restricted as in tragedy,
wore masks of a grotesque kind, special footwear called the
comic sock and often had a phallic emblem. Their costumes
were extravagantly padded.

The only surviving comedies of the fifth century representing
what was subsequently called by the ancients the Old Comedy
are nine plays by Aristophanes. A further two plays by Aristophanes of a slightly different character survive from the early
fourth century. The first most striking feature of Old Comedy is
the satirical character and the ridiculing invective against named
individuals, whether politicians like Pericles and Cleon, philosophers and thinkers like Socrates, or poets like Euripides. Many
other individuals (whose significance is often lost upon us now)
are also named, including notable or newsworthy characters of
the city presumably present in the audience. Hence the verb
komodein, meaning to represent in comedy, is also used in this
period to mean to satirise, ridicule, lampoon or libel. A second
striking feature is a persistent and frank indecency with regard to
sexual matters and bodily functions. In *Lysistrata*, for example,
when the women of Athens and Sparta agree to bring the war to
an end by withdrawing their sexual services until peace is
concluded, the menfolk are in an acutely priapic state for
much of the play.

Aristophanic laughter acts as a kind of release from normal
social embarrassment and inhibition. Most plays involve some
extravagant fantasy: the *Birds*, for example, concerns an attempt
to establish an ideal city in the sky ('Cloudcuckooland') where
the inhabitants can rule by controlling the food supply of both
men and gods, who are also treated irreverently in Aristophanic
comedy. Despite the fantastic and highly imaginative elements, a
realistic picture of the life of the ordinary Athenian citizen
emerges through the distortion of the comic lens. In the *Wasps*
and *Assemblywomen* we can see how the system works. Hence the

100

anecdote that when the philosopher Plato was asked by the tyrant Dionysius of Syracuse about the Athenian constitution, his reply was to send him the plays of Aristophanes. A notable formal feature is the *parabasis*, in which the poet uses the chorus to break the dramatic illusion midway through the play to speak in his own voice, sometimes to harangue the spectators with advice of topical import that may or may not be connected with the issues of the play. Like tragedy, comedy is a poetic form, and many of the choral lyrics have an appealing delicacy and charm. Together with singing and dancing the chorus (particularly the animal choruses) doubtless provided an extravagant visual spectacle, so that considered as a whole, Aristophanic comedy is a remarkably varied and lively phenomenon the like of which the world has never quite seen again.

The *Knights*, the first play produced by Arisophanes himself in 424, is a quite savage attack upon the leading politician of the day, Cleon, Pericles' successor as leader of the Athenian *demos*, who had recently gained political kudos by his presence at a notable Athenian victory over the Spartans at Pylos in 425. In the person of Cleon, the general political leadership of Athens is being attacked. At the end of the play the imperialist schemes of Hyperbolus (such as the conquest of Carthage) are denounced, as is the general Athenian tendency to swindle the allies and prosecute the war at all cost.

An oracle is discovered that Cleon, a seller of leather by trade, is to be ousted from the favour of Demos (the Athenian people) by a sausage seller. One comes along and when told of his destiny feels unworthy because he was born in the gutter, has no virtues to speak of and can scarcely read or write. When told: 'Come off it, you don't think politics is for the educated do you or the honest? It's for the illiterate scum like you now!' (ll. 191–3), he is still doubtful, wondering how he can arrange the affairs of the city. He is then reassured: 'Dead easy; just carry on what you've always done. Mix all the city's policies into a complete hash, butter the people up a bit, throw in a pinch of rhetoric as a sweetener, and there you are' (ll. 213–16). He is supported by the chorus of Knights or cavalrymen, who as men of education and social standing are the natural opponents upstarts from the *nouveaux riches* such as Cleon.

Cleon arrives and a furious shouting match (the contest, or *agon*) develops between them. The sausage seller contends that

101

he is a bigger crook than Cleon; he has been cheating his customers in the market (the *agora*, which can also mean assembly) for years. They compete for the favour of the irascible and stupid old man Demos by flattery, bribes and interpretation of oracles. The sausage seller points out that, though a tanner, Cleon has never given Demos a pair of shoes, and he provides him with a pair as well as a tunic and a chair for his comfort. Just before the final contest, old Demos in conversation with the Knights shows that he isn't quite as simple as he seems. He knows the thieving ways of politicians. Then there is a contest of hampers to appeal to Demos' appetite; the sausage seller, by a clever trick he uses on his customers, is able to steal Cleon's jugged hare while he is distracted, and wins by showing Demos that while his hamper is empty, Cleon has kept much of the food for himself (with the clear implication that the real Cleon lines his own pockets). Cleon now confesses that he has been outdone in shamelessness and sees the truth of the oracle. The sausage seller is now revealed as Agoracritus, 'the choice of the assembly' or 'market haggler'. 'In the *agora* I thrived on wrangling' (ll. 1257–8). This fits the sausage seller both as purveyor of meat in the market place and as citizen of Athens schooled in the ways of the world in the assembly. In the wordplay here is concentrated the wit and design of the whole play. There may also be a third meaning: 'I fed myself in the agora in judging' (in the law courts where in the developed democracy a citizen could earn three obols a day, a living wage. Here may be adduced the remark in the *Gorgias* of Plato, 'People say that Pericles made the Athenians lazy and cowardly and garrulous and covetous by his introduction of the system of payment, for services to the state' (575e).).

Then, following Medea's example, the sausage seller boils Demos to rejuvenate him so that he appears as he was in the good old days of Miltiades, the general who had commanded the Athenians in their finest hour when they had defeated the Persians at Marathon. Demos is then amazed at his stupidity and vows to reform the politics and manners of the city. He is pleased to be shown two sweet 30-year-old treaties (in female form presumably) whom Cleon had hidden away and whom Demos can take back to his farm in the country. In a neat reversal Cleon is given Agoracritus' old job, selling sausages (a mixture of dog and donkey) at the city's gates.

As Cleon had successfully prosecuted Aristophanes a year

earlier for bringing the city into disrepute before foreigners, the *Knights* was a defiant reply, as the *parabasis* makes clear. Aristophanes judged the audience well, for the judges awarded him first prize. Addressing the judges in the *Assemblywomen*, the poet has this suggestion to offer: 'Let the intellectuals choose me for my intellectual content; to those who enjoy a good laugh, judge me on my jesting. That should get most of the votes' (ll. 1155–7). Those who came simply for the entertainment doubtless enjoyed seeing their leaders brought down to size, revelling in the caricature, the burlesque and the reduction to absurdity. In the Athenian democracy Jack was as good as his master, or perhaps the Jacks had taken the place of the master. The more discerning doubtless appreciated the playwright's wit in pressing the resemblance between the politician who sells himself and the sausage seller haggling in the market place and indulging in a spot of male prostitution on the side (l. 1242).

The comparison entails a withering political analysis that is not wholly mitigated by the general air of mirth and absurdity or by the wishful ending. The clear implication is that Demos gets the politician he deserves. As for Aristophanes' relation to the real Athenian *demos*, this may be likened to the jester at the court of the king; he is allowed the fool's licence to insult them with the unflattering truth. Paradoxically, the *Knights* may be said to be a tribute to the maturity of the Athenian democracy (Cleon, of course, continued to be popular, and Aristophanes to attack him, to his death in 422) as well as a stringent criticism of it, as damning in its way as that of Thucydides in his history or that of Plato in his *Republic* and unlike these delivered directly at the time when the criticism might evoke a response.

The relation between dramatic art and life is subjected to a serio-comic critical scrutiny in the *Frogs*, written just after the death of Euripides and at a time of impending national disaster in 405. Newly arrived in Hades, Euripides by his sophistical talents has greatly impressed the riff-raff he encounters there and as a result attempts to usurp the throne of tragedy from the incumbent Aeschylus, who furiously resists. A contest ensues in which their poetry is to be weighed. Dionysus (a comic god in this play), who has gone down to Hades for love of Euripides' poetry, is to be judge.

The chorus characterises the poets in language appropriate to their actual styles: Aeschylus will sweep all before him in a grand

manner thundering in anger with mighty words and grandiloquent maxims; Euripides will side-step the bombardment with
his subtle analysis, clear-cut phrases and neat wit, refining,
dissecting and finding fault. Euripides is the sophist who prays
to strange gods and finds his opponent Olympian, obscure,
bombastic, lacking in dramatic action and artistically primitive; Aeschylus is the traditionalist who accuses his opponent
of degrading tragedy in subject matter and style with his
importation of kings in rags, incest on the stage, subtle argumentation and common talk. Euripides takes pride in having
slimmed tragedy of its excess weight. He has given a voice to
women and slaves and made tragedy truly democratic. He has
taught his audiences to speak, to look into things, to be critical,
to follow subtleties in plot, and showed them scenes from
common life. He has encouraged the spirit of enquiry.

Aeschylus begins his attack by asking Euripides what he thinks
is the purpose of poetry: 'wit, wisdom and to make the people
better citizens' replies Euripides (ll. 1009–10), Aeschylus then
points to the difference between the patriotic citizenry of his day,
inspired by warlike plays such as the *Seven against Thebes* and the
Persians, and the idle men of the *agora* of the present, who prefer
talking and debating to wrestling and sport. Euripides has done
harm by bringing on to the stage things better kept concealed,
like the story of Phaedra. It is the duty of poets to talk of
wholesome things and to be useful in the tradition of
Orpheus, Musaeus, Hesiod and Homer.

Though the ponderous lines of Aeschylus easily prevailed in
the weighing ceremony, Dionysus likes both poets equally and
finds it difficult to judge between them. As he wants to bring
back a poet to save the city, he asks their advice about the
current critical situation of 405. Shall Alcibiades be recalled
from exile? The gnomic utterances are characteristically clever
(Euripides) and obscure (Aeschylus). Dionysus tries again. What
are we to do? Euripides says (as Aristophanes had said more
openly and forcefully in the *parabasis*) that they must trust new
men. Aeschylus, being out of touch, asks what sort of men the
city must put its faith in, the good and the true? Of course not,
says Dionysus. Aeschylus then doubts whether the city can be
saved. Nevertheless, Dionysus finally chooses Aeschylus, a choice
endorsed in a famous ode as follows:

Aeschylus is returning to earth to the joy of the citizens because of his sound understanding and intelligence. For it is right not to sit beside Socrates indulging in idle talk, ignoring the Muses and stripping the tragic art of its most essential aspects. To waste time on solemn arguments and petty quibble is the part of a fool.

(ll. 1491–9)

Is this an aesthetic judgement or a moral criticism, or both? And is it directed against Euripides or those who are left in Athens and follow his example without his talent? The jesting at Euripides' expense seems to be affectionate, and in judging the play account must be taken of its tone, which is not always easy to pin down. But since the word used by the chorus for idle talk (*lalein*) is also used by Euripides when he claims to have taught people to speak (l. 954), we are doubtless meant to make the obvious connection, even though it is clear that Aristophanes does not represent Euripides as any more of a fool than Aeschylus. For the figure of the older poet is equally comic; he emerges as an irascible old fogey, even if he is the spokesman for the values of the old world that Aristophanes had wistfully evoked in the wishful ending of the *Knights*. That Aristophanes took his didactic office seriously is clear from the seriousness of the *parabasis*, though it would be foolish to accredit a sophisticated and subtle spirit like his with naive views about the ability of poets to reform (or conversely to corrupt) mankind.

Nevertheless, these words of the chorus have often been taken very seriously indeed as summing up Aristophanes' belief in a genuine cultural malaise that had spread through Athens with dire political consequences. Written as they were just after the death of the last great tragic poet and just before the defeat of Athens in 404, from which she never recovered her former pre-eminence, they have been seen to be prophetic of the decline in imaginative creativity to come in the fourth century. The current malaise and future decline are put down to the new critical spirit of the Greek enlightenment, represented here by Socrates and to some extent Euripides. In fact, of course, though similarly sceptical of received ideas, they responded very differently to the new critical spirit. The hostility later shown to tragic poets (including Aeschylus) by Socrates as Plato's spokesman in the

Republic (see p. 137) has further given the comic poet's analysis here the uncanny force of prophecy.

LATER COMEDY

The last two plays of Aristophanes, the *Assemblywomen* and *Wealth*, differ from their predecessors in that the *parabasis* is abandoned and the plays are less overtly political. The fantastic and the anarchic yield just a little to probability and realism in character and plot construction. In an earlier play, the *Thesmophoriazusae*, the burlesque of Euripidean recognition scenes, cunningly contrived escapes snatching the victim from the jaws of death and ingenious plotting points to the new direction that comedy was gradually to take in the fourth century until it is quite transformed in the plays of Menander (*c.* 342–293). Indeed, there are more links between the New Comedy and Euripides (if we take what are sometimes called his later romances, *Ion*, *Helen* and *Iphigeneia in Tauris*, with their intrigues, coincidences and the poetic justice of their happy endings) than between Old and New Comedy. Wit, indecency and caricature give way to humour, decorum and the realistic presentation of typical characters, the realism being such as to have prompted a famous question 'O Menander, O life, which of you imitated the other?' The New Comedy of general manners is no longer political, that is intimately concerned with public affairs and the workings of the city state, which has now lost its independence in the greater Macedonian empire.

In addition to substantial fragments, one complete play by Menander survives, the *Dyskolos* ('The Peevish Man'), which was performed in 316. It has a five-act structure, a chorus that is no more than a musical interlude between acts and a prologue figure as in Euripides to set the scene. The central character is an obstacle in the way of the young man who has fallen in love at first sight with his daughter. Only when he has been rescued from near death after falling down a well does the peevish old man (who is much tormented by a garrulous cook and an impertinent slave) learn the error of his ways: 'Only disasters can educate us' (ll. 699–700), and accommodate his misanthropy to the common-sense norms of social living. Likewise, the young man is put to the test to prove himself worthy of the happy marriage that awaits him at the play's end. The New Comedy depends for its effect upon the clever manipulation of the stereotypical, whether this be of characters like the boasting soldier, the shameless bawd, the manipulative slave and the stern father, or of plot devices like recognition by means of rings and necklaces, substitution of children and mistaken identity. It does not challenge the audience but confirms the norms of a bourgeois world. Through Roman imitation it has greatly influenced modern European drama.

ORATORY AND PROSE

Although the historians and philosophers are treated primarily in chapters devoted to history and philosophy, Herodotus, Thucydides and Plato are masters of Greek prose who might equally claim a place here for their literary qualities. Aristotle's extant works lack polish; his more stylish work does not survive. The earliest of them, Herodotus, writes in an easy, familiar style that has affinities with the oral tradition. Indeed, his language has been described as 'speech as it is spoken'. But by the time of Thucydides, prose writing had been affected by the new study of rhetoric associated with the sophist movement that reached Athens in the generation after Herodotus. The earliest rhetoricians seem to have emanated from Sicily, and rhetoric made a powerful impact at Athens with the visit in 427 of the Sicilian sophist Gorgias of Leontini (*c.* 485–375), famous for his use of antithesis, balance and parallelism in length of clauses and sounds of words.

Oratory itself had long played a part in Greek life, in the courts (forensic), in the assembly (deliberative) and on festive occasions (epideictic), but through the systematic study of rhetoric, the sophists and their successors sought to put the art of speaking and speech-writing on a more professional basis, equipping their pupils for success in the public life of the developed *polis*. In the fourth century, rhetoric became the centrepiece of schools orientated more towards practical learning than the philosophical Academy of Plato or the later Lyceum of Aristotle. The founder of one such school, the Athenian Panhellenist Isocrates (436–338), voices his thinking on this topic in his festival oration the *Panegyricus* (46):

Philosophy took a part in the discovery and development of all these, and gave us education in the field of affairs and civilised relations with each other. . . . Our city showed the way to it, and also gave honour to skill in words, which is the desire and envy of all. She realised that this alone is the particular and natural possession of man, and that its development has led to all other superiorities as well. She saw that other activities showed such confusion in practice that wisdom was often the way to failure in them, and folly to success, while good and skilled powers of speech were outside the scope of the ordinary people, but were the province of the well-ordered mind: and that in this respect wisdom and ignorance are furthest apart, and the birthright of a liberal education is marked not by courage, wealth and similar distinctions, but most clearly of all by speech, the sign of which presents the most reliable proof of education, so that a fine use of words gives not merely ability at home, but honour abroad. Athens has so far outrun the rest of mankind in thought and speech that her disciples are the masters of the rest, and it is due to her that the word 'Greek' is not so much a term of birth as of mentality, and is applied to a common culture rather than a common descent.

Plato was distrustful of rhetoric and of the teaching of the sophists because he felt that they were not grounded in the quest for truth. In the dialogue *Gorgias*, for example, he shows Socrates refuting the sophist Gorgias, who asserts that rhetoric is the most important of human concerns because successful statesmanship relies not on knowledge of the good but upon the art of persuasion. Nevertheless, in the education system of Greece, it was rhetoric rather than philosophy that came to be central, and this continued to be the case at Rome and in the Renaissance.

The art of rhetoric affected not only oratory but all kinds of prose composition; similarly the analysis of prose in antiquity is invariably rhetorical. A useful introduction here is provided by the analysis of the Greek rhetorician Dionysius of Halicarnassus (*fl.* 30) who wrote essays on various Athenian orators and a substantial work entitled *On Composition*. At the beginning of an essay on Demosthenes, he cites the account of *stasis* from Thucydides quoted above (p. 61) as an example of the grand style. It is strikingly elaborate because the style is remote from normality and much embellished; it can startle the mind, induce

tension or strain and express violent emotion. Dionysius com-
mends Thucydides for his ability to represent the terrible, the
remarkable and the pathetic. He distinguishes four characteristics of his style: artificiality of vocabulary, variety of figures,
harshness of word order and rapidity of signification (*Thucydides*, 24). Though he does not eschew pleasing rhythms, he is
often abrupt, varying his constructions in unexpected combina-
tions and so jarring the ear and surprising the mind. Later in the
same essay, Dionysius describes Thucydides' style as austere and
archaic, one that aims at dignity rather than elegance (*Thucydides*,
38–9). In translation, Thucydides appears smoother in English
than he does in Greek, but comparison of the account of *stasis*
with passages from other prose writers cited below will bear out
some of Dionysius' main points.

At the other end of the scale from Thucydides, Dionysius sets
the style of Lysias (*c*. 459–380), exemplifying the plain style. A
number of Lysias' orations survive, mostly forensic in character,
and he is regarded as the finest example of the pure Attic stylist.
In an essay devoted to him, Dionysius distinguishes a number of
characteristics including his use of the ordinary vocabulary of the
speech of his day (unlike Thucydides, he does not use archaisms),
the expression of ideas in this everyday language without much
use of metaphor, and the ability to reduce ideas to essentials with
lucidity and terseness of expression. These may seem humdrum
virtues but Dionysius praises him as a fine literary artist who can
conceal his art in the production of stylish melodious prose.

> Rhythm is a not unimportant factor in prose: it is not to be
> classed as an inessential adjunct, but to tell the truth, I
> consider it to be the most potent device of all for bewitching
> and beguiling the ear.
>
> (*Demosthenes*, 39)

Melody cannot be represented in translation, but his other
qualities may be suggested by the concluding paragraph of the
speech *Against Eratosthenes*, one of the thirty oligarchs who ruled
Athens at the time of her defeat in 404–403.

> However, I do not intend to talk of what might have been
> when it is beyond me to describe the truth of what was
> perpetrated, which would be beyond the scope of any
> number of accusers. But there has been no slackening in

my eager regard for our temples, which they sold or dese-
crated, for our city, which they brought low, for our ship-
yards, which they destroyed or for the dead, whom they
failed to protect in their life and whom you must avenge
after their death. I believe these dead are listening to what
we say, and will know that you are making your vote, and
feel that every vote of not guilty will be a vote for their own
condemnation, every vote of guilty one of retribution on
their behalf.

The style is easy yet formal, lucid yet patterned, simple and
smooth yet morally intense.

Having established the styles of Thucydides and Lysias as
touchstones for the grand and the plain respectively, Dionysius
distinguishes a third style that is a mixture of the two, which he
variously calls the middle, the mixed or the well-blended. The
classical exponents of this are Plato and Isocrates. Though
paying general homage to Plato's writing, Dionysius is not
particularly illuminating in the actual examples he cites. However, the treatise *On the Sublime*, traditionally attributed to the
rhetorician Longinus and perhaps written in the first century AD,
contains suggestive appreciations of Plato's highly figured style.

Now although Plato . . . flows with such a noiseless stream,
he none the less achieves grandeur. You are familiar with his
Republic and know his manner. 'Those, therefore,' he says,
'who have no experience of wisdom and goodness, and are
always engaged in feasting and similar pleasures, are
brought down, it would seem, to a lower level, and there
wander about all their lives. They have never looked up
towards the truth, nor risen higher, nor tasted of any pure
and lasting pleasure. In the manner of cattle, they bend
down with their gaze fixed always on the ground and on
their feeding-places, grazing and fattening and copulating,
and in their insatiable greed for these pleasures they kick
and butt one another with horns and hoofs of iron, and kill
one another if their desires are not satisfied.'

(13)

Longinian sublimity is not to be equated with Dionysius'
conception of the grand style; the sublime is that moving quality
in great literature that has the capacity to take us out of

ourselves in *ekstasis*, in ecstasy; passages that have this effect on diverse people in diverse times can be called truly sublime. Such passages may be written in what Dionysius calls the grand style, or the mixed or the plain style. This passage from Plato is highly figurative in the modern sense that tends to restrict the word to signify imagery. Ancient rhetoricians, as the work of Dionysius suggests, paid as much attention to figures of sound and arrangement (the Gorgianic figures, for example, like antithesis and isocolon) as to figures of sense and meaning (metaphor, simile, metonymy, etc.). It may seem ironic that Plato, who distrusted rhetoric and feared the power of poetry to the extent that he banished most forms of poetry from his ideal *Republic* (see p. 137), should himself be the most poetical of philosophers, famous throughout the ages for his imaginative presentation of ideas. His style in the Socratic dialogues is rooted in familiar conversation that is designed to be comprehensible to the general reader – he avoids jargon or technical terms – while at the same time they are designed to make philosophy palatable and to entice the hearts and minds of the sceptical. To this end, he uses many picturesque analogies and vivid images of illustration, as in the above example. Nevertheless, Plato always exerts the kind of rigid control over his own poetic powers that he required of poets in his ideal state, who are to write not with an eye to pleasure but in an austere style that can be useful (*Republic* 398a). Much of the beauty of his style stems not so much from the invention of images as from the judgement with which he applies them. This is nowhere more true than in the case of his most famous image, the allegory of the cave in the *Republic* (514) discussed in chapter 4.

Dionysius' second exemplar of the middle or well-blended style is Isocrates. His diction is elegant and smooth; his clauses are arranged in parallel both in syntax and sound within gracefully rounded periods which flow continuously without any abruptness or hiatus in sense or sound, for the general aim is euphony and musical effect. He cites an elegant passage from *On the Peace* (41) contrasting the attitudes of the Athenians of his day towards threats from abroad with the conduct of their heroic ancestors at the time of the Persian Wars.

Now what if a stranger from abroad were to come and suddenly find himself embroiled in our affairs, before having the time to become corrupted by our depravity: would he not think us insane and beside ourselves, when we glory in the deeds of our ancestors, and think it right to sing the city's praises by recounting the achievements of their day, and yet act in no way like them but do exactly the opposite? For, whereas they waged ceaseless war on behalf of the Greeks against the barbarians, we expelled from their homes those who derive their livelihood from Asia and led them against the Greeks; and whereas they liberated the cities of Greece and came to their aid, and so earned the right to be their leaders, we try to enslave them and feel aggrieved when we are not honoured as they were. We fall so far short of the men of those times in both our deeds and our aspirations that, whereas they had the courage to leave their country in order to save Greece, and fought and conquered the barbarians on both land and sea, we do not see fit to run any risk, even for our own gain, but seek to rule over all mankind, though we are unwilling to take the field ourselves for this but employ instead stateless men, deserters and fugitives who have come together as the result of other crimes and who, whenever others offer them higher pay, will follow their leadership against us.

Dionysius praises the purity of Isocrates' diction, his precision in idiom, his clarity of expression and the shapely structure of his sentences, but he also finds cause for criticism in the lack of concision and in the sluggishness of effect. He feels that his style can be circumlocutionary, repetitious and long-winded. He criticises Isocrates for timidity in the use of metaphor, for sacrificing intensity and emotion to mellifluousness of effect, and for a lack of variety in his use of figures, most especially in his exhausting predilection for parallelisms and antitheses.

These comments, indeed much of what has been said about Lysias, are by way of prelude and preamble to the main subject of the essay in which they occur, Demosthenes, who in Dionysius' verdict is the supreme orator, combining, in an eclectic style, the virtues of all the various styles he has described, while avoiding their various limitations: the obscurity that can be a deficiency in Thucydides, the lack of emotional vigour that can characterise Lysias, the lack of variety and the diffuseness sometimes present in Isocrates. He juxtaposes with the passage from

112

Isocrates an extract from Demosthenes on a similar theme, remarking 'He does not set out each separate pair of actions in finicky detail, old and new, and compare them, but carries the whole antithesis through the whole theme by arranging the items in two contrasting groups thus' (*Demosthenes*, 21).

Yet observe, Athenians, what a summary contrast may be drawn between the state's achievements in the time of your ancestors and in your own day. The tale will be brief and familiar to all; for you need not look abroad for examples that provide the key to your future prosperity, but at home, Athenians. Our forefathers, whose speakers did not humour or caress them, as those of today do you, for forty-five years ruled the Greeks with their consent; they accumulated more than ten thousand talents in their treasury; the king of that land submitted to them, as a barbarian should to Greeks; they set up many glorious monuments to commemorate victories won by their own fighting on land and sea; and they alone among mankind have left behind them a reputation which envy cannot erase. Such were their achievements in Hellenic affairs: now see what they were like in their domestic affairs, both as citizens and as men. In public they erected for our benefit such a wealth of beautiful buildings and other objects, such as temples and the dedicated objects in them, that posterity has been left no chance to surpass them. In their private life they were so moderate, and adhered so steadfastly to the national tradition, that anyone who knows the style of house which Aristides had, or Miltiades, or other famous men of that day, is aware that it was no grander than his neighbour's. They did not engage in politics for personal profit, but each felt it his duty to enrich the commonwealth. By conduct honourable towards the other Greeks, reverence towards the gods and fair dealing in domestic matters, they deservedly achieved great prosperity.

That is how the state fared of old under the statesmen I have mentioned. How is it faring now under the worthies of the present day? Is there any similarity of resemblance? I pass over many topics on which I could wax eloquent; but with the dearth of competition which you all observe, the Spartans being in eclipse, the Thebans being fully occupied and none of the rest capable of challenging us for supremacy, it should be possible for us to hold our own securely and arbritrate the claims of others. Yet we have been deprived of territory which belongs to us, and have spent more than one thousand five hundred talents to no purpose; these politicians have lost in peace time those allies which we gained in war, and we have trained up a formidable enemy to fight against us. Or let anyone come forward and tell me where else Philip has obtained his power, if not from us. 'Well, my dear sir, you may say, if our foreign affairs are in a bad way, at any rate things at home are better now.' What possible proof is there of this? The parapets we whitewash? The roads which we repair? The fountains and the other nonsense? Look at the statesmen who are responsible for these: some have risen from beggary to opulence, or from obscurity to honour; some have made their private houses more splendid than public buildings, and their wealth has increased at the same pace as the fortunes of the state have declined.

(*Olynthiac*, III, 23 ff.)

Dionysius admires Demosthenes' greater variation in clauses, sentence structure and figurative arrangement. He is not tied to one manner or style. But above all it is the end result of all these technical effects, the greater energy and vehemence of feeling, that he admires. He goes on to say that while Isocrates puts him into a tranquil and serious frame of mind, Demosthenes transports him through a whole series of emotions.

Feeling and elevation are what Longinus illustrates in a short passage from Demosthenes in which the orator seeks to assure the Athenians that they were right to oppose Philip of Macedon at Chaeronea even though they were defeated.

Demosthenes is putting forward an argument in support of his policy. What was the natural procedure for doing this? 'You were not wrong, you who undertook the struggle for the freedom of the Greeks, and you have a precedent for this here at home. For those who fought at Marathon were not wrong, nor those at Salamis, nor those at Plataea.' But when, as though carried away by the inspiration of Phoebus himself, he uttered his oath by the champions of Greece, 'By those who stood the shock at Marathon, it cannot be that you were wrong', it would seem that, by his use of this single figure of adjuration, which I here give the name of apostrophe, he has deified his ancestors by suggesting that we ought to swear by men who have died such deaths as we swear by gods; he has instilled into his judges the spirit of the men who stood there in the forefront of the danger, and has transformed the natural flow of his argument into a passage of transcendent sublimity, endowing it with the passion and the power of conviction that arise from unheard-of and extraordinary oaths. At the same time he has infused into the minds of his audience words which act in some sort as an antidote and a remedy, so that, uplifted by these eulogies, they come to feel just as proud of the war against Philip as of the triumph at Marathon and Salamis.

(16)

Longinus and Dionysius, both late products of the rhetorical tradition which they seek to illuminate, help us to see that just as the great sculptures could not have come to be without scientific study and technical mastery systematically acquired over a long period of time, so the great artistic achievements in Greek oratory and prose in the late fifth and fourth centuries presuppose gradual development of a scientific awareness of language and psychology of a kind systematised by Aristotle in his *Rhetoric*.

THE ALEXANDRIAN AGE

Owing to its museum and library, Alexandria soon became the literary capital of the Hellenistic world. The literati, working in a rarefied scholarly atmosphere that was very different from that of the classical *polis*, wrote for a cultivated audience delighting in artifice. A few of the surviving texts may indicate the range of literary production.

The *Phaenomena*, a didactic poem of over 1,500 lines on the constellations by Aratus (*c.* 313–*c.* 240), reflects the Alexandrian interest in science. The *Idylls* of Theocritus (300–260), short poems of about 100 to 150 lines long, featured several in which shepherds with elegant names competed with one another in mellifluous song set in the beautiful landscape of Sicily where Theocritus had grown up. The sophisticated city poet nostalgically recreating a romantic image of the simpler rural world of his boyhood thereby created the pastoral genre. The beautiful 'Lament for Bion', attributed to the later, second-century poet Moschus uses the pastoral convention to pay poetic tribute to the deceased poet as shepherd. In Idyll I, Theocritus' shepherd Thyrsis sings a lament for the mythical herdsman Daphnis, who is apparently dying for love, in lines that have been famously echoed in subsequent pastoral elegies.

> Where were you Nymphs, when Daphnis came to grief?
> What distant valley or mountain gave you delight?
> You could not be found beside Anapus, the great river,
> Nor by the water of Acis, nor on Etna's height.
>
> Muses, sing for a herdsman, sing me your song. . . .
>
> Bear violets now, you bramble bushes and thorntrees,
> Let the world turn cross-natured, since Daphnis dies.
> Let the prickly juniper bloom with soft narcissus,
> The pine be weighed with pears. Let the stag hunt the
>   hounds,
> Let the nightingale attend to the screech-owl's cries.
>
> Goodbye to the herdsman, Muses, goodbye to the song.

In the seventh Idyll, 'Harvest Home', is a sensuous evocation of a Mediterranean landscape, vivid in sight and sound.

> There, happy in our welcome, we flung ourselves down
> On couches of fragrant reeds and freshcut vineleaves.
> Above our heads a grove of elms and poplars
> Stirred gently. We could hear the noise of water,
> A lively stream running from the cave of the Nymphs.
> Sunburnt cicadas, perched in the shadowy thickets,
> Kept up their rasping chatter; a distant tree-frog
> Muttered harshly as it picked its way among thorns;
> Larks and linnets were singing, a dove made moan,
> And brown bees loitered, flitting about the springs.
> The tall air smelt of summer, it smelt of ripeness.
> We lay stretched out in plenty, pears at our feet,
> Apples at our sides and plumtrees reaching down,
> Branches pulled earthward by the weight of fruit.

This suggests the rich pictorial appeal of Theocritus' poetry.

Theocritus also wrote short mythological poems in the genre subsequently called *epyllion*, or brief epic. The *Argonautica* of Apollonius of Rhodes (*c.* 295–*c.* 215), a romantic epic in four books, is the first to give prominence to love, which is treated with delicate psychological insight. Callimachus (*c.* 305-c.240) wrote *Hymns* in a learned allusive style. In the first century Meleager collected together a large number of short poems from various authors and periods in his *Garland*. Epigrams by Meleager and others featured in the *Greek Anthology*, a Byzantine compilation including many short poems of this period.

To the scholars of the Alexandrian library, one of the most famous of whom was Aristarchus (*c.* 217–*c.* 145), noted for his work on Homer, the world is indebted for the preservation of the Greek classics in reasonably good textual order. Texts were standardised and methods of copying improved. Doubtless standards were set here that influenced the copying of texts and book production throughout the ancient world.

4

PHILOSOPHY

It is through wonder that men now begin and originally began to philosophise; wondering in the first place at obvious perplexities, and then by gradual progression raising questions about the greater matters too, e.g. about the changes of the moon and of the sun, about the stars and about the origin of the universe. Now he who wonders and is perplexed feels that he is ignorant (thus the myth-lover is in a sense a philosopher since myths are composed of wonders); therefore if it was to escape ignorance that men studied philosophy, it is obvious that they pursued science for the sake of knowledge, and not for any practical utility.

Aristotle, *Metaphysics* I, 2, 9

THE PRESOCRATICS

The very word philosophy, meaning in Greek the love of wisdom, suggests what the world owes to the Greeks. The first thinkers consciously to reject the account of the world handed down in the traditional myths emanated from Ionia in the seventh and sixth centuries. The movement from myth to philosophy was perhaps made easier by the nature of the myths themselves. In the *Iliad* Zeus is not omnipotent or omniscient, nor did he create the world. He shares his power with other gods and took power himself from his father. He is subject to laws beyond his own will, recognising that he cannot save his son Sarpedon from fate (XVI, 433–61). The Homeric concept of fate might suggest a topic for speculation to the enquiring mind.

Little of the Presocratic writing survives except for quotations in later authors, but by common consent the earliest Ionian thinker was Thales of Miletus, who was born in the latter half of the seventh century. He believed that the primary substance from which everything came into being and of which all is ultimately made is water. Other Ionian philosophers came to different conclusions about the primordial substance, but their common enquiry was into the nature of the physical universe on the assumption that it is both one and intelligible.

Pythagoras in the second half of the sixth century marks a reaction against the materialism of the early Ionians. He migrated from Samos in Ionia to southern Italy where he founded a community for initiates on religious lines. Associated with Pythagoras is the doctrine of the soul's immortality and its reincarnation in a cycle of lives in the animal and human spheres (metempsychosis). The body is regarded as the prison or tomb of the soul, which may be purified in an ascetic life of study. He explained the universe not in physical but in metaphysical terms, tracing the origin of all things to number. He is accredited with developments in mathematics and music, in particular with the doctrine of the harmony of the spheres, which in their motion were supposed to make heavenly music. With Pythagoras the word *kosmos*, which means good order or decency in early Greek, is first used to describe the perfect order and arrangement of the universe.

Heraclitus of Ephesus of the late sixth and early fifth centuries expressed the belief that fire is the primordial substance. The world is an everlasting fire which is partly flaring up and partly dying down in equal measure so that a continuous balance is maintained. Essential to this balance are tension and strife in which all subsists. Unlike other Ionian materialists, he associated this primordial element with the *Logos*. This universal reason, the principle whereby there is unity in diversity and diversity in unity, is divine and all-wise and is to be identified with what is eternal and constant, the One, while the phenomenal world is constantly changing and in a state of flux.

Parmenides of the Eleatic school (Elea was a Greek colony in southern Italy) in the fifth century believed that Being, the One, is real while Becoming, change, is illusion. He distinguished two ways of apprehending the world. There is the way of truth in which there is knowledge of Being, which, for Parmenides, is material and the way of opinion (the common condition of

119

ordinary men and women) that takes the world of Becoming as real. The mutable world of appearances that we apprehend through the senses is unreal; Being is the only true object of knowledge and is known through reason and thought.

These and other early philosophers are collectively known as the Presocratics, because, with Socrates philosophy takes a new direction. The Roman writer Cicero (106–43) made the famous remark that Socrates first brought philosophy down from the skies to the common problems of mankind (*Tusculan Disputations*, V, 4, 10). This may be taken to mean that philosophy moved from physics to ethics. This change, though associated with Socrates, may be seen as a consequence of a greater shift gradually taking place in Greek culture as a whole. Between the earliest speculations of the Presocratics and the time when Socrates had come of age in about 450 came the full flowering of Attic tragedy, in which practical human problems and questions of a philosophic, religious and ethical nature are raised and debated in dramatic form. Sometime before Socrates' maturity, Herodotus had published his *Histories*, a work symptomatic of an adventurous pioneering spirit of enquiry into the human world and one that extended beyond the Greek horizon. Developments in philosophy may be seen as a natural accompaniment or consequence of other imaginative and empirical explorations; together they are complementary aspects of the growing Greek enlightenment.

SOCRATES (469–399) AND THE SOPHISTS

Socrates did not write anything, so that our knowledge of him comes principally from two sources, from the historian Xenophon (*c.* 428–*c.*354) who wrote personal recollections of him in his *Memoirs of Socrates*, and chiefly from the philosopher Plato (*c.* 427–347) who made Socrates his chief spokesman in his dialogues, all written sometime after Socrates' death in 399. How far the historical Socrates is accurately represented by the Platonic Socrates has long been a matter of debate. When even historians like Thucydides put words into the mouths of leading figures (see p. 59), there is no reason to suppose that Plato felt constrained by the need to preserve historical accuracy in the portrayal of his master. Most scholars believe that Socrates did not develop any system of beliefs and that what the world has come to know as

Figure 12 Delphi: theatre and site of the temple of Apollo, one of the spiritual centres of the Greek world. On the portal of the temple which housed the famous oracle (consulted by Socrates) were inscribed the words *gnothi seauton*, Know Thyself, and *meden agan*, Nothing in Excess

Platonism, although expressed through the Platonic Socrates, is an extension by Plato of tendencies in Socrates' thought.

The historical Socrates, the son of an Athenian stonemason in whose trade he was trained, is above all associated with the *method* to which he has given his name, the origin of which is given in the *Apology*, an early dialogue in which Plato has Socrates tell how his friend Chaerophon had consulted the oracle at Delphi to ask whether there was any one wiser than Socrates. The oracle replied 'No'. Dumbfounded at this, Socrates set out to refute the oracle by seeking out those with reputations for wisdom, the philosophers, poets and artists, only to find that they knew nothing at all, but, unlike Socrates, did not recognise their own ignorance. Thereafter he considered it his duty to disabuse all sorts and conditions of men of their own self-conceit and their own self-ignorance, and so put them on the road to truth. His favourite method involved cross-questioning; for this he pretended to be ignorant in order to draw out and

121

refute an opponent. The Greek word for this kind of pretence is *eironeia* and this questioning method is called Socratic irony (see the *Republic*, 337a). The refutation is generally called the *elenchos*. By destroying the conceit that we already have knowledge, the *elenchos* is negative in effect, destructive of self-ignorance, conventional beliefs and received opinions: the effect of it is perplexity or impasse, *aporia* in Greek. But our sources are agreed in stressing the integrity of Socrates and in showing that, as an instrument of his probing intelligence, the Socratic method served a positive moral function in paving the way for clarity of thought about moral issues.

In a famous analogy, Plato makes Socrates compare his mission and his method to that of his mother, who was a midwife:

> But I have this feature in common with midwives – I myself am barren of wisdom. The criticism that's often made of me – that it's lack of wisdom that makes me ask questions, but say nothing positive myself – is perfectly true. Why do I behave like this? Because the god compels me to attend to the labours of others but prohibits me from having any offspring myself. I myself therefore am quite devoid of wisdom; my mind has never produced any idea that could be called clever. But as for those who associate with me – well, although at first some of them give the impression of being pretty stupid, yet later, as the association continues, all of those to whom the god vouchsafes it improve marvellously, as is evident to themselves as well as to others. And they make this progress, clearly, not because they ever learn anything from me; the many fine ideas and offspring they produce come from within themselves. But the god and I are responsible for the delivery. . . . When I ask a question, set about answering it to the best of your ability. And if, on examination, I find that some thought of yours is illusory and untrue, and if I then draw it out of you and discard it, don't rant and rave at me, as a first-time mother might if her baby were involved. . . . I do what I do because it is my moral duty not to connive at falsehood and cover up truth.
>
> (*Theaetetus*, 150c–151b)

The Socrates who is midwife to truth does not seek, like earlier philosophers, to impart truth from without, nor does he seek merely to destroy old beliefs: his midwifery serves a positive function in bringing new birth, as each individual mind becomes self-aware and seeks the ground of its own conviction.

The doctrine which seems to have been the ground of Socrates' actual beliefs is expressed in the proposition that virtue (*arete*, excellence) is knowledge. The wise man who knows what is good and what conduces to human happiness will do what is good and conduces to human happiness. Wrong actions are a result of a faulty perception of what conduces to true human good. It is possible to learn (and therefore in a sense to teach, but the 'teacher' can only be midwife to truth) what conduces to true human good and happiness, and, once learnt, the knowledge will be irresistible. Hence it is possible to say that no one willingly does wrong. His ethical concern did not of course lead Socrates to prescribe rules for good conduct, but was directed towards the increase of self-awareness as a prerequisite to the health and well-being of the *psyche* (spirit or soul, including the mind).

The enquiring method of Socrates is one of the first fruits of the great intellectual change that manifested itself throughout the Greek-speaking world in the second half of the fifth century, sometimes known as the Greek enlightenment. The same period saw the growth of a new kind of professional teacher throughout Greece. These men were called sophists, a name derived from the word for wisdom or skill, *sophia*. They moved from city to city, giving lessons in such things as mathematics, politics and the art of public speaking, designed to be useful for the rising political classes. The name of Gorgias of Leontini, an Ionian colony in Sicily, is associated with the development of rhetoric and examples survive of his highly antithetical style, which is thought to have influenced Thucydides. Protagoras of Abdera in Ionia is accredited with the famous saying 'man is the measure of all things', often understood to imply a doctrine of relativity in relation to knowledge and scepticism as to the universality of any science. About the gods he was agnostic. He is said to have been the first to propose that on every subject there can be two conflicting opinions. He features in a dialogue of Plato that bears his name, where he is treated respectfully and debates with Socrates various questions relating to politics, pleasure and knowledge. He exhibits common sense and at one stage offers an account of his purposes as a teacher:

When he comes to me, Hippocrates will not be put through the same things that another sophist would inflict upon him. The others treat their pupils badly; these young men, who have deliberately turned their backs on specialisation, they take and plunge into special studies again, teaching them arithmetic and astronomy and geometry and music . . . but from me he will learn only what he has come to learn. What is that subject? The proper concern of his personal affairs, so that he may best manage his own household, and also his state affairs, so as to become a real power in the city, both as a speaker and man of affairs.

(Protagoras, 318d–e)

Plato draws a sharp distinction between Socrates and the sophists, whom he represents as men who taught skills without genuine interest in moral truth or in the higher ends which knowledge should be made to serve. Certainly there is a gulf between the practical aim of worldly success expressed by Protagoras here and the divine mission of Socrates. In method they differed too. The sophists gave lectures in schools for a fee; Socrates did not give lectures nor did he set up a school or take fees.

Nevertheless, when Aristophanes satirised the sophists in the *Clouds* of 423, he chose Socrates as the representative of the new learning. An elderly farmer called Strepsiades ('The Twister') has heard of Socrates, as a man who can make the worse case appear a better one, and hopes to profit from his teaching to cheat those to whom he is in debt. He goes to the 'thinking school' of Socrates where he is introduced to the clouds, whom Socrates alleges to be responsible for producing rain rather than Zeus. (There is a tradition that Socrates began with physics before turning to ethics.) But Strepsiades is too stupid to learn anything, so he sends his son Pheidippides instead. The son hears the unjust argument defeat the just argument, and as a result of the new learning is able to teach his father to cheat his creditors. But he then beats his father, proving that he is justified in doing so and disowns the authority of the gods. Strepsiades sets fire to Socrates' school in disgust.

The comic indictment of Aristophanes proved to be uncannily prophetic. In 399, in the restored democracy, Socrates was put on trial on the serious charge of corrupting the minds of the young and of believing in deities of his own invention instead of the gods recognised by the city. Plato makes Socrates refer to the Aristophanic caricature in the defence he gave at his trial:

> Very well, what did my critics say in attacking my character? I must read out their affidavit, so to speak, as though they were my legal accusers. Socrates is guilty of criminal meddling in that he inquires into things below the earth and in the sky and makes the weaker argument defeat the stronger, and teaches others to follow his example. It runs something like that. You have seen it for yourselves in the play by Aristophanes where Socrates goes whirling around proclaiming he is walking on air and uttering a great deal of other nonsense about things of which I know nothing whatsoever.
>
> *(Apology,* 19b–c)

Those who brought the charge probably wished to punish Socrates for his criticism of democracy (made on the grounds that government should be in the hands of experts whereas the *demos* is undisciplined and untrained) and his supposed influence upon the likes of Alcibiades, who had sought to undermine the Athenian democracy from without. At his trial Socrates refused to employ a proper defence, choosing instead to make an honest and uncompromising avowal of his life's aims and endeavours:

> Perhaps someone may say, But surely, Socrates, after you have left us you can spend the rest of your life in quietly minding your own business. This is the hardest thing of all to make some of you understand. If I say that this would be disobedience to god, and that is why I cannot 'mind my own business', you will not believe that I am serious. If on the other hand I tell you that to let no day pass without discussing goodness and all the other subjects about which you hear me talking and examining both myself and others is really the very best thing that a man can do, and that life without this sort of examination is not worth living, you will be even less inclined to believe me.
>
> *(Apology,* 37e)

Condemned to death after his conviction by 281 votes to 220, he refused to escape from prison, but chose to drink hemlock in the traditional manner, showing a cheerful courage and a philosophic calm in the face of death, as recorded in Plato's *Phaedo*.

The testimonies to the character of Socrates written after his death by Xenophon and Plato are designed in part to vindicate him against the charges of his detractors. Plato puts his most extended formal eulogy into the mouth of Alcibiades in his *Symposium*, written about 385 but set in 416 before the Sicilian expedition when Alcibiades was still in good repute. Towards the end of the *Symposium*, a drinking party at the house of the tragic poet Agathon in which the participants each give a speech in praise of love (*eros*), Alcibiades bursts in and announces that the only encomium he will give will be of Socrates himself, whom he likens to the figures of Silenus in statuaries' shops; their unprepossessing exterior belies their inner reality, for they are hollow inside and when opened up can be seen to contain little figures of the gods. In mythology, Silenus is a pot-bellied, sleep-prone drunkard who in sober waking moments dispensed wisdom to those who could pin him down and constrain him to do so. The flesh-and-blood Socrates was fat, ungainly, snub-nosed and ugly, not at all the image of the dignified philosopher that has come down to us in the idealised busts of Plato and Aristotle, in which the physical and intellectual are harmoniously blended in the typical Greek way. He was the butt of comedians and into this comic portrait fits the figure of his second wife Xanthippe, an archetypal shrew who gave her husband a bad time. Alcibiades also likens him to Marsyas the satyr, who can entrance men with his flute: Socrates casts his spell simply with his words and speech. Then comes the confession of Alcibiades, which might be thought to be Plato's answer to Socrates' detractors:

> He compels me to realise that I am still a mass of imperfections and yet persistently neglect my own true interests by engaging in public life. So against my real inclination I stop up my ears and take refuge in flight, as Odysseus did from the Sirens.

> (216a)

Only Socrates has induced in him a feeling of shame.

He then exposes the Silenus figure, with the observation that Socrates (like all the Athenians present at the banquet) has a tendency to dote on beautiful young men and (unlike his fellows) pretends to be ignorant and know nothing:

But this is exactly the point in which he resembles Silenus; he wears these characteristics superficially, like the carved figure, but once you see beneath the surface you will discover a degree of self-control (*sophrosyne*) of which you can hardly form a notion, gentlemen. Believe me, it makes no difference to him whether a person is good-looking – he despises good looks to an almost inconceivable extent – nor whether he is rich nor whether he possesses any of the other advantages that rank high in popular esteem; to him all these things are worthless, and we ourselves of no account, be sure of that.

(216d–e)

As proof of his self-control, Alcibiades then tells a remarkable story. As a handsome young man he deliberately set out to offer himself to the older man in fulfilment of the ideal set out elsewhere in the *Symposium*, in which male love (assumed by all the speakers to be alone capable of fulfilling the highest and noblest aspirations) becomes ideal when it inspires the search for truth and beauty. Alcibiades goes to the extent of getting into bed with Socrates, who sleeps with him for the night. We are not to suppose that Socrates is not tempted, but he chastely remains immune to the young man's charms. The anecdote is designed to illustrate, without solemnity, Socratic *sophrosyne*: the divine inner being masked by the comic exterior. For Alcibiades, it is both an insult and a revelation of Socrates' strength of mind and character further confirmed in the famous incident in which he walks barefoot on ice in the wintry siege of Potidaea. Further testimony follows of his courage as a soldier of Athens, of his endurance and of his essential indifference to the needs of the senses. Though a great drinker, no one has ever seen him drunk. There is the story of his extraordinary trance-like withdrawal into thought, an inner concentration that lasted a day and a night. Little wonder that Alcibiades finds him absolutely untypical, indeed unique (221c).

The final part of the encomium stresses the extraordinary quality of his talk:

I forgot to say at the beginning that his talk too is extremely like the Silenus-figures which take apart. Anyone who sets out to listen to Socrates talking will probably find his conversation utterly ridiculous at first; it is clothed in such curious words and phrases, the hide, so to speak, of a hectoring Satyr. He will talk of pack-asses and blacksmiths, cobblers and tanners, and appear to express the same ideas in the same language over and over again so that any inexperienced or foolish person is bound to laugh at his way of speaking. But if a man penetrates within and sees the content of Socrates' talk exposed, he will find that his talk is almost the talk of a god, and enshrines countless representations of ideal excellence and is of the widest possible application.

(221d–222a)

Xenophon and Plato represent him as patriotic and law-abiding. They record his respect for the state religion. In their accounts, his mission is laid upon him by the Delphic god, and his famous *daimonion*, the inner voice which acted as a warning sign, is regarded as being of divine origin. For Xenophon he was the best and happiest of men: pious, just, self-controlled, sensible (*Memoirs of Socrates*, I, 11). After recounting his death in his dialogue the *Phaedo*, Plato pronounces him to have been of all whom they knew in their time, the best, the wisest and the most upright man (*Phaedo*, 118). Plato's tribute culminates in the superlative form of the adjective *dikaios*, which is related to the noun *dikaiosyne*, justice or righteousness, the sum of the four cardinal virtues of the ancient world, including courage, wisdom and temperance. In his life and in his manner of dying, Socrates embodied for his admirers the perfection of the philosophic spirit.

PLATO (*c.* 427–347)

Born of aristocratic parents in around 427 in Athens, Plato wrote poetry in his youth before turning to philosophy, notably when he encountered Socrates. In the *Republic*, written about 375 but set in earlier times, the main respondents of Socrates, Glaucon and Adeimantus, are the elder brothers of Plato, who must have sat at the feet of Socrates and learned his philosophy in a similar way. After Socrates' trial and death in 399, he turned aside from the political career he had contemplated and travelled extensively. He visited the court of the tyrant Dionysius I of Syracuse and met the ruler's brother-in-law Dion, with whom he struck up a friendship. In his seventh letter, written to friends of Dion after his death, Plato records that his experience in Athens had convinced him that good government was only possible if philosophers became kings or if by some miracle kings became philosophers. Plato returned to Athens and began teaching in a school situated in the grave of a hero named Academus, hence the school was called the Academy. It seems that he hoped the Academy might be a nursery for philosopher kings, and the school attracted the sons of the powerful and wealthy from all over the Greek world. When Dionysius I died in 367, Dion invited Plato back to Syracuse to train the new young ruler Dionysius II, who was not, however, a responsive pupil.

Plato is the first systematic thinker in western philosophy, though the surviving Platonic dialogues (some thirty in number) featuring Socrates as the main speaker (in all but one or two late works) are not a systematic exposition of his philosophy as it was taught in the Academy. There is some evidence, if Plato is indeed the author of the letters that have been attributed to him (there is dispute about this among scholars) that he deliberately refrained from committing his more advanced thoughts to paper. The dialogues seem rather to have been designed for popular consumption, to be fully intelligible to the general reader throughout, without the use of technical language. As to the recreation of the character of Socrates long after the historical figure had died, Plato is hereby affirming the soundness of his methods and seriousness of his mission as an educator of mankind and midwife to truth: the Platonic Socrates is an imaginative extension of the real figure and a dramatic embodiment of the philosophic spirit in action, a model of the kind of man who believes (and acts on the belief) that virtue is knowledge.

The dialogues are therefore exemplary, but they are also meant to be enticing. In the *Symposium*, for example, Plato clearly wishes to cast the kind of spell over his readers that Alcibiades says Socrates habitually cast over those with whom he conversed. In the realistic presentation of an actual drinking party we see 'the feast of reason and the flow of soul'. The fully human setting, conjured up by Plato's literary art, is what has given the Socratic method its irresistible appeal. Moreover, however much they may ascend to the ideal, the discussions all start in the real world of practical human concerns.

It is not only the setting over which Plato takes pains. When he introduces Aristophanes in the *Symposium*, the comic poet speaks very much in character (one to which Plato seems well disposed), offering an entertaining fantasy in which Zeus cut the original human beings in half to punish them, with the result that love is the search for the lost half, 'the desire and pursuit of the whole' (189–93). What starts as a joke after the more scientific lecture delivered by the previous speaker proves to be the most thought-provoking speech of the first half of the colloquium, in the best serio-comic Aristophanic style. There is a pointed contrast of character in the *Republic*, when, after the polite and careful cross-questioning of the sweetly reasonable Socrates, the abrupt denunciation of him by the opinionated and dogmatic sophist, Thrasymachus, comes as a dramatic surprise (336b). The portrayal of him is deliberately extreme; the contrasting example of the sophist throws the superior qualities of Socrates' mind, motive and method into clear relief.

A key to the whole tendency of Plato's thought, in particular to the sharp distinction he makes between the ideal and the phenomenal world, can be found in the famous allegory of the cave in the sixth book of the *Republic* (513e–518). This is a graphic representation of the tendency in Greek thought to find the source of human happiness and virtue in knowledge and to exalt the wise man as the enlightener and saviour of mankind, opening up the possibility of a steep and arduous upward road to truth through the application of human intelligence and the exercise of the power of reason.

The allegory of the cave is designed to be a figurative illustration of Plato's theory of knowledge. Socrates has been arguing that the true philosopher is not content to study a variety of beautiful objects, but seeks to know what beauty is in itself, what is called the 'form' (*eidos*) or 'idea' (*idea*) of beauty (476).

In Plato's theory there are forms of abstract things, like beauty, goodness and justice, and of physical things, like beds and tables. These forms transcend the phenomenal world of sense impression, that is the world that we perceive through our senses of sight, hearing, touch, smell and taste. They exist apart and are eternal and unchanging. The phenomenal world in some way participates in this greater transcendent world of forms: a beautiful object is informed by beauty itself; a bed shares in the non-physical reality of the ideal bed. Only the forms are the

DIAGRAM ILLUSTRATING ELEMENTS OF PLATO'S THOUGHT

The upward road to truth through philosophic enlightenment

The Divided Line	The Allegory of the Cave
A *noesis* (understanding)	The Sun (the form of the good)
Intelligence of the forms, having understanding of ultimate reality of the form of the good, the ground of all hypotheses and assumptions.	Grown accustomed to the light, the eyes can view the sun. As the sun gives visibility to the objects of the sensible world and the power of seeing to the mind, so the good gives the power of knowing to the mind.
B *dianoia* (reasoning)	
Mathematical intelligence dealing with underlying realities but in a deductive way that is uncritical of assumptions.	The prisoners released from the cave must accustom their sight to the new reality and begin by looking at shadows and reflections of real things.
episteme (knowledge) Above the line	Outside the cave: sunlight

---

Below the line *doxa* (opinion)	Inside the Cave: firelight
C *pistis* (belief)	
True opinion informed by knowledge but held on trust. Commonsense views of things without understanding of first principles underlying the mutable world of sense impression and experience.	Freed slaves turn towards the fire and see the objects that cast the shadows. These objects (still artificial) are believed to be real.
D *eikasia* (illusion)	
Shadows and reflections taken to be real. Second-hand opinions and impressions Poetry and the images of art belong to this realm. So does the teaching of the sophists, who simply make a science out of common opinion.	Fettered slaves view shadows of objects cast by firelight as real. The state of ordinary men and women.

Figure 13   The elements of Plato's thought in the *Republic*

131

objects of true knowledge. He who apprehends merely the particularities of the phenomenal world, apprehends mutable appearances, what seems to be true. He does not have knowledge, but has opinion (*doxa*: the Greek word has the same root as the word *dokein*, to seem). The ultimate end of knowledge is the form of the good, which gives meaning and value to everything in the universe. When asked to be more precise about this supreme reality, Socrates confesses that he is unable to be so, and resorts to figurative language for further illustration, comparing the form of the good to the sun which gives visibility to the objects of the sensible world and the power of seeing to the eye. So the good makes the objects of thought (the forms) intelligible and gives the power of knowledge to the mind (506d–509c). Plato then explores the distinction between the visible and intelligible worlds with the analogy of the divided line, through which he clarifies four sharply distinct mental states (the figure clarifies since in life they might not be so independent of one another). Opinion can be informed and true, or illusory and false; knowledge may be of ultimate reality (the forms), or of a lesser reality, which nevertheless transcends the world of sense (mathematical propositions).

Then comes the allegory of the cave. The prisoners in the cave have been fettered since childhood in their underground cave and can only look in front of them. They have one fixed view, from which they can see reflected on the wall opposite shadows of objects being carried through the cave by men walking on a road above them, in front of which a wall has been built. Above and behind the road is a fire, whose light casts the shadows of the objects, which may be figures of men or animals in stone. For the prisoners, the shadows are the only realities. If one of them is let loose and compelled to turn his head and walk towards the fire, faced with the passing objects, he will resist the new reality, taking refuge in the familiar. The light of the fire will hurt his eyes. If he is forced to make the ascent to daylight, the process will be painful and he will at first not be able to see what is pointed out to him as real. Until his eyes grow accustomed to the light, he will look at shadows and reflections, then at objects themselves, then at the heavens by night. The last thing he will be able to look at will be the sun itself. Then he will come to realise that the sun is the cause of all things. Reflecting upon his former life, he will see that it was worthless. If he is made to come back to the cave, he will again be blinded and make a fool of himself in the eyes of his former fellows, who will think the ascent has destroyed his eyesight and is not worth making. If anyone attempts to release them they will try to kill him.

Socrates likens the ascent into the upper world to the progress of the mind into the intelligible realm. The final perception is of the form of the good, which is the cause of all things right and true (517b–c).

In passing, it may be noted that another aspect of this ascent is the ascent of the ideal lover on the ladder of beauty, from the beautiful objects of the physical world on the lower rung, to the beauty of the soul and on to the beauty of abstractions, like laws and institutions, until he finally ascends to contemplation of the form of beauty itself, an incommunicable mystical experience that is the climax of the prophetess Diotima's speech to Socrates on the nature of *eros* in the *Symposium* (210–12).

Ordinary earthly life is lived in a benighted condition of ignorance from a fixed point of view, in which the deluded soul is imprisoned, without knowing it, in a world of transient shadows. The impeding fetters are not simply intellectual, but are also moral. Nothing short of a radical turn-around of our mental and moral nature is needed. Enlightenment is a slow and painful process that is naturally and powerfully resisted by the ignorant and blind. Each stage of the upward journey into light is painful and difficult. But enlightenment is possible; eventually the released prisoner can behold the sun, although he is reluctant and has to be compelled at every stage. When in the beginning, after he has turned his head, he is told that all he has previously seen is illusory and he is cross-questioned about the objects passing before him, he is at a loss (in *aporia*), believing what he saw previously to be more real. The unmistakable allusion here to the Socratic method of refutation of conventional opinion (the *elenchos*), makes it clear that only the philosopher can effect the reformation necessary for enlightenment, though it is a dangerous proceeding, for the ignorant prisoners are liable to kill the man who attempts to lead them up the steep ascent.

Given the bleak picture of unreformed human life in the allegory, it is not surprising that Socrates concludes that the philosopher, with his eye on the good, will be reluctant to involve himself in human affairs and may make a fool of himself if he is put on trial in the lawcourts, where the shadow of justice prevails. The *Republic* itself is an attempt to envisage the reformation necessary in social arrangements if justice is to flourish in the individual and the community. Socrates recognises that the ideal state is a pattern laid up in heaven which anyone can find and establish in himself (592b). At the same time, without the ideal environment, he clearly feels that the individual effort will meet with the greatest difficulty.

The nature of the ideal state is defined in carefully argued stages, but in the final blueprint, the city, which will be an aristocracy based on merit, will be divided into three classes, the chief of which is the class of guardians, the philosophic rulers, whose orders will be carried out by the second class of auxiliaries. The third class constitutes workers, whether farmers or business men. The guardians, who may be male or female, are not allowed to own property or handle money. Their needs are to be provided for by the rest of the community. All women are to be held in common to all men, and children are to be held in common to be brought up in state nurseries. No child shall know its parents; no parent shall know its own child. There will be mating festivals, at which rulers will arrange for the best men to mate with the best women, in a rigged ballot to avoid dissent, with the object of ensuring that the best offspring results. The conflict of interest between the family and the state will therefore be eliminated. The state will be one large family and so have maximum unity. In the *Assemblywomen* of 392 (written before the *Republic*), Aristophanes makes a comedy of arrangements similar to these.

The ideal state will embody the four cardinal virtues of wisdom, courage, temperance and justice. Its wisdom, *sophia*, will reside in the guardians, its courage, *andreia*, in the auxiliaries, and its temperance, *sophrosyne*, in the harmonious acceptance of the order of the state by all three classes. Justice, *dikaiosyne*, is the principle that makes this temperance possible; it is the extension of the principle of the division of labour upon which society is based in the first place, the principle whereby each class fulfils its own function without trespassing on the functions of the other two.

The nature of the state reflects the nature of the individual writ large. The individual soul is made up of three parts, corresponding to the three classes in the state: the rational part, the spirited part and the appetitive part. The wisdom of the individual resides in the rational part, courage in the spirited part and temperance in the harmonious relation between the three parts, specifically in the way in which the lower parts consent to the rule of reason. A comparison may be made here with the famous passage in the *Phaedrus* (253d–255) in which the division of the soul into three parts is represented by a charioteer driving two horses, one noble, the other wanton, each pulling in opposite directions. Justice in the individual, as in the state, is the principle whereby each part of the soul fulfils its own function without interfering with the functions of the other two. Justice is therefore the harmony and health of the soul.

Plato's idealism in the *Republic* leads him to a very negative view of the existing form of democracy. Indeed he has been seen as the enemy of liberal and humanitarian ideals and the prophet of totalitarianism. After he has established the philosophic state based on the rule of reason, Socrates in Book Eight distinguishes four kinds of unjust states, each representing a progressive decline, as the rule of reason is usurped by the lower elements in the psyche. First comes timocracy, meaning the rule of honour (the Spartan state is an example), in which the spirited element rules without the tempering guidance of philosophy. Then comes oligarchy, the rule of the few, in which honour has given way to the love of riches as the ruling principle. The people rebel in the name of liberty and equality, but democracy inevitably degenerates into anarchy and licence where the lowest elements in the psyche predominate. Democratic man becomes a prey to extravagant and unnecessary appetites, living from day to day and satisfying every whim without any ruling principle. A faction-ridden democracy easily degenerates into tyranny, where all are enslaved to the ruling passions of a single man. In the allegory of the cave, the clear allusion to the death of Socrates associates the democracy of his day with brutal ignorance from which Plato recoiled, but which was also the spur that led him to conceive the *Republic* and his other Socratic dialogues as a defence of all that Socrates had lived and died for. The writing of these dialogues itself exemplifies the moral duty that Plato laid upon the philosopher to descend again into the cave for the purpose of attempting conversion of the ignorant rather than being content to cultivate his own garden or rest assured within the walls of an enlightened Academy of his own making.

Equally notorious is Plato's hostility to poetry, though he
himself has always been considered to be the most poetical of
philosophers, a judgement arising from the harmony and proportion of his prose style, which is enriched by the imaginative
presentation of ideas through picturesque analogies, developed
allegories like that of the cave or the use of myth to push
philosophical enquiry beyond the point at which certain knowledge is possible, as in the myth of Er at the end of the *Republic*, in
which he graphically represents the doctrine of the immortality
of the soul and its reincarnation.

Much of the discussion of the preliminary education of the
guardians is concerned to modify the existing Greek programme, in which poetry and mythology played a significant
part. His treatment of the two go hand in hand, since he believed
that traditional mythology was largely the invention of the poets.
He does not banish poets and their stories altogether (the word
for story is *mythos*), but poetry that tells lies about the gods or
shows heroes in a bad light, encouraging emotional excess in
those who read it, is condemned on moral and theological
grounds. Here Plato is renewing the objections of previous
philosophers, for the battle between poetry and philosophy
had been going on since the early Ionian philosophers attacked
the view of the world (and especially of the gods) in the poems of
Homer and Hesiod (607b). Poetry on suitable subjects and myths
that are morally edifying continue to play a leading part in the
education of the young (376e, 399b). Indeed, in the ideal state,
all the inhabitants, including the guardians, are to be persuaded
of the truth of a foundation myth which Plato calls a noble
fiction (sometimes translated as 'noble lie', for he uses the
same word, *pseudos*, for fiction and falsehood, 414b–415d).

The existing pattern of Athenian education consisted of
mousike paideia, relating not only to music but to all the arts
over which the nine Muses presided (including literature, history and all the liberal arts), and *gymnastike paideia*, physical
education. They were designed to complement one another
and produce the all-round individual. Plato envisages reform
of this education to ensure that aesthetic development and a
strong moral sense run parallel. This preliminary education of
the guardians, which is designed to promote harmonious development of character rather than to reach true knowledge, is to
be followed by the study of mathematics, astronomy and

harmonics, not for any practical value but for the training of the mind. The motto 'Let no one who is ignorant of mathematics enter here' was inscribed over the doors of the Academy. The theorems and hypotheses of mathematics represent the reflections of real things seen by the prisoners of the cave in the water, after they have been newly released into the blinding light. Mathematical study leads to a knowledge of greater reality than anything in the world of sense, and so is the best way of leading the mind upward to a vision of the highest order of reality, the forms that are known through dialectical reasoning (532c–d).

Plato objects to poetry as a mode of truth because it is a representation (*mimesis*, sometimes translated 'imitation') of the world of appearances, which is itself a distorted reflection of the transcendent world of unchanging and eternal forms. The images of the poet (for which Plato's word is *eikones*) are at two removes from reality, so that poetry belongs to the lower realm of *eikasia* (usually translated as 'illusion') in which shadows and reflections are mistaken for reality by the ignorant prisoners in the darkness of the cave. Poetry must yield to the higher reality of philosophy. Hence the famous judgement which shows Plato deeply at variance with traditional Greek culture:

> when you meet people who admire Homer as the educator of Greece, and who say that in the administration of human affairs and education we should study him and model our whole lives on his poetry, you must feel kindly towards them as good men within their limits, and you may agree with them that Homer is the best of poets and first of tragedians. But you will know that the only poetry that should be allowed in a state is hymns to the gods and poems in praise of good men; once you go beyond that and admit the sweet lyric or epic muse, pleasure and pain become your rulers instead of law and the rational principles commonly accepted as best.
>
> (606e, 607a)

ARISTOTLE (384–322)

Born in 384 at Stagira where his father had been court physician to the Macedonian king, Amyntas III, Aristotle was sent to the

Athenian Academy of Plato in 367, where he studied until Plato's death in 347. He then left Athens to direct his philosophical studies abroad. In 343/2 he was invited by King Philip to the Macedonian capital Pella to tutor his 13-year-old son Alexander. Anecdotes report that the philosopher prepared a special edition of Homer for the edification of his illustrious pupil. He returned to Athens in 335 where he opened a new school to rival the Academy in the Lyceum, a gymnasium in the temple of Apollo Lyceus, located in a grove just outside the city. From his habit of providing instruction in the *peripetos* or covered walkway of the gymnasium, the school has often been called Peripatetic. With the death of Alexander in 323 and the Greek revolt against his subordinates, Aristotle, with his well-known Macedonian connections, withdrew from Athens to avoid prosecution. He died in Chalcis in Euboea in the following year.

While the extant corpus of Plato's writings are polished literary works for public consumption and none of his Academy lectures survives, Aristotle's polished writing in dialogue form has been lost and what survives is mostly in the form of lecture material used in giving courses at the Lyceum. The surviving esoteric treatises may in some cases be notes taken by pupils, and have all been assembled and edited by later Aristotelians. For example, his *Metaphysics* is regarded as a series of small treatises on various philosophical problems, put together and given its title because it was to be read after the *Physics* (the literal meaning of meta-physics). This has had the effect of making Aristotle's philosophy seem more of a system than it doubtless was, and modern Aristotelians have found development, change and sometimes contradiction within our surviving texts.

After Plato, what is immediately striking is the great range of Aristotle's intellectual interests. He continues to reflect the Socratic and Platonic emphasis upon the moral and metaphysical, but is less theoretical and mathematical than Plato, extending the range of his philosophical enquiries to the physical and particularly to the biological. He starts from observed phenomena, believing that man achieves knowledge by looking outward, as well as inward, and by maintaining contact with the world of sense impression. His physics concerns not abstractions but real substances as they move and change spontaneously. This empiricism is most evident in his biological work. We cannot imagine the other-worldly and visionary Plato devoting time to (and doing the research for) the classification of biological phenomena according to structure and function that we find in several of Aristotle's works, including his monumental *History of Animals*, in which we see the natural philosopher reaching out towards a clear definition of the actual world and towards an explanation of facts.

In Aristotle, for the first time, the various branches of learning and science are systematically classified, differentiated and defined, so that subsequent developments in logic, physics, metaphysics, zoology, political and moral science, psychology, rhetoric and literary criticism all grow out of Aristotelian beginnings. While Plato eschewed technical terms in his popular writings, to Aristotle the world owes a whole philosophical vocabulary and grammar, so to speak. The 'vocabulary' comprises categories and essential terms such as form and matter, energy and potential, substance and essence, quantity and quality, accidental relations and causes, genus and species. The 'grammar' comprises Aristotelian logic (from *logos* meaning word, discourse or reason, something distinctive to the human species), for he saw the necessity of establishing rules for correct argumentation, in the course of which he became the first to analyse sentences, bequeathing the terms subject and predicate amongst others. Later commentators entitled his logical works the *Organon* or 'tool', recognising that Aristotelian logic is not an end in itself but the indispensable prerequisite to any fruitful scientific enquiry.

While Plato is an idealist, Aristotle is often called the first great representative of the realist school of western philosophy. The reaction against Plato and his greater realism may be illustrated in his critical appraisal of Plato's *Republic* in his own *Politics* (1260–4). He finds fault with Plato's proposals to abolish the family and ownership of private property among the ruling guardians, which he believes to be neither practical nor desirable. He attacks the basic premise from which Plato argues that the highest unity of the state is its highest good, insisting that plurality is the nature of a state. He argues that Plato does not take into account the facts of human nature; present evils and abuses in society spring not from private ownership and the family, but from basic human wickedness. He also finds gaps in Plato's provisions, noting that there are no arrangements for the majority, the third class of artisans and farmers. Contemplating the class structure of Plato's city, Aristotle sees two states in one, a recipe for strife. Arguing that the whole cannot be happy unless all or at least some of its parts are happy, he finds fault with Plato's argument that the happiness of the guardians is to be sacrificed to the happiness of the whole, clearly believing along with Glaucon (*Republic*, 419) that Plato's ideal city will be a dismal place to live in. He himself, working empirically from an analysis of 158 existing constitutions, classified governments under three headings: rule by the single person, rule by a few and rule by the many. The first would be the ideal, but the corruption of it into tyranny is the worst of all. Similarly, rule by the few will easily degenerate into a self-seeking oligarchy. Though he had more faith in the collective judgement of the *demos* than Plato, he favoured reform of extreme democracy to incorporate various checks and balances. In the best polity, faction will be avoided if there is a strong middle class (*Politics*, 1295–6).

More radically, Aristotle came to reject the stark dualism of Plato's theory of ideas. He agreed with Plato's rejection of the insistence of the Presocratics that the primordial substance was material, and accepted that the basic reality consisted of forms, but denied that these forms exist apart from the sensible world. The form is not transcendent but is immanent in the individual and the particular. The form and its essence cannot exist apart from the things whose form and essence they are. In rejecting the theory of ideas, he also rejected the belief that went with it, which Plato had inherited from the Pythagoreans, that the body is the prison of the *psyche* or soul.

In his own work *On the Soul* (*psyche*, which is better thought of as the animating principle), Aristotle does not allow that, as far as earthly life is concerned, the body and the soul are two substances pulling in different directions and that the soul's purpose is to struggle free from the bonds of matter. Body and soul are one:

> Let us go back again as from the beginning in the attempt to define what the soul is and what might be the most general account of it. One kind, then, of the things that there are we call *substance*, and part of this group we say to be so as matter [*hyle*], that which is not in itself a particular thing, a second part we say to be so as shape [*morphe*] or form [*eidos*], in

accordance with which, when it applies, a thing is called a particular, and a third as that which comes from the two together. Now matter is potentiality [*dynamis*] and form is actuality [*entelecheia*] . . . soul is substance as the *form* of a natural body which potentially has life, and since this substance is actuality, soul will be the actuality of such a body.

(*On the Soul*, II, 1)

Later he calls the soul the cause (*aitia*, 'the reason for') or first principle of the living body, its final cause. We believe that we possess scientific knowledge of a thing when we think we know its cause. We must acquire knowledge of original causes, of which there are four: the material, the formal, the efficient (what makes something come to be) and the final (the end which it serves, from *finis*, the Latin word translating *telos*, whence teleological, and meaning 'end'). If we take the example of a house, the material cause tells us about the material of which it is constructed; the formal cause tells us of the structure or the plan of the house; the efficient cause tells us what is necessary for the building of the house, such as the art of building and design; the final cause tells us about the function of the house (see e.g. *Physics*, II, 3, 24). These famous Aristotelian distinctions represent a new clarity and definition in relation to previous thought about causation.

The four causes apply equally to natural things.

Hence, if it is by nature and also for a purpose that the swallow makes her nest and the spider his web, and that plants make leaves for the sake of the fruit and strike down (and not up) with their roots in order to get nourishment, it is clear that causality of the kind we have described is at work in things that come about or exist in the course of Nature.

(*Physics*, II, 8, 25)

Nature is a 'principle of movement and change'. The movement is always the realisation of an end, the actualisation of an original potentiality. Aristotle's thought is therefore thoroughly teleological. As there is a final so there is a first cause. 'So inasmuch as motion [*kinesis*] is eternal, it follows that the prime mover, if it be single, or the prime movers, if plural, must likewise

141

be eternal' (*Physics*, VIII, 6, 8). The Unmoved Mover exists in a state of eternal contemplation.

What then is the final cause of man? What is his purpose or his end? What is peculiar to man is that which distinguishes him from the vegetable and animal worlds, his rational faculty enabling rational activity:

> Let us take it that what we are concerned with here is the reasoning power in action for it is generally allowed that when we speak of 'reasoning' we really mean *exercising* our reasoning faculties . . . . The function of a man is the exercise of his non-corporeal faculties or 'soul' in accordance with, or at least not divorced from, a rational principle . . . . The good for man is 'an activity of soul in accordance with goodness' or (on the supposition that there may be more than one form of goodness) 'in accordance with the best and most complete form of goodness.'
>
> (*Ethics*, 1, 7)

Aristotle's word for goodness and virtue here is *arete*, which may better be translated as excellence:

> Virtue, then, is of two kinds, intellectual and moral. Of these, the intellectual is in the main indebted to teaching for its production and growth, and this calls for time and experience. Moral goodness, on the other hand, is the child of habit, from which it got its very name, ethics being derived from *ethos*, 'habit', by a slight alteration in the quantity of the *e*. This is an indication that none of the moral virtues are implanted in us by Nature, since nothing that Nature creates can be taught by habit to change the direction of its development.
>
> (*Ethics*, 11, 1)

Education, the responsibility of the city, is to play a vital role in the inculcation of good habits. As we acquire the moral virtues by first exercising them, so Aristotle is persistent in stressing that virtue is a matter of action:

> For in 'doing well' the happy man will of necessity *do*. Just as at the Olympic games, it is not the best looking or the strongest men present who are crowned with victory, but competitors – the successful competitors – so in the arena of

human life, the honours and rewards fall to those who show
their good qualities in action.

(Ethics, I, 8)

In the *Ethics*, Aristotle does not attempt to legislate for virtue
(excellence, *arete*); he lays down no rules to be followed, no ten
commandments or prescriptions for the good life, recognising
that in discussing right conduct in action he is dealing with an
inexact science:

> Now matters of conduct and consideration of what is to
> our advantage have no fixity about them any more than
> matters affecting our health. And if this be true of moral
> philosophy as a whole, it is still more true that the discus-
> sion of particular problems in ethics admits of no exacti-
> tude. For they do not fall under any science or professional
> tradition, but those who are following some line of conduct
> are forced in every combination of circumstances to think
> out for themselves what is suited to those circumstances,
> just as doctors and navigators have to do in their different
> *métiers*.

(Ethics, II, 2)

He then advances the most famous general principle of his
Ethics:

> Let us begin with the following observation. It is in the
> nature of moral qualities that they can be destroyed by
> deficiency on the one hand and excess on the other. We
> can see this in the instances of bodily health and strength.
> Physical strength is destroyed by too much and also by too
> little exercise. Similarly health is ruined by eating and
> drinking too much or too little, while it is produced, in-
> creased and preserved by taking the right quantity of drink
> and victuals. Well, it is the same with temperance, courage,
> and the other virtues. The man who shuns and fears every-
> thing becomes a coward. The man who is afraid of nothing
> at all, but marches up to every danger, becomes foolhardy.
> In the same way the man who indulges in every pleasure
> without refraining from a single one becomes incontinent. If,
> on the other hand, a man behaves like the Boor in comedy
> and turns his back on every pleasure, he will find his
> sensibilities becoming blunted. So also temperance and

courage are destroyed both by excess and deficiency, and they are kept alive by observation of the mean.

(*Ethics*, II, 2)

The doctrine of the mean has become something of a commonplace, but the discussion and application of it in the *Ethics* are subtle and discriminating. The philosopher shows us how inadequate our judgements about the virtues can be and how, both in our acting and in our judging, we must be perpetually flexible in our moral insight.

Aristotle introduced his definition of man in order to define the nature of happiness ('living well or faring well') for which the Greek word is *eudaimonia*, the desired end of all human activity. Happiness is not to be equated with pleasure, though pleasure will be a part of it, nor with fame (though his 'high-souled man' has a just regard for his own reputation: Ethics, IV, 3), nor even with moral excellence, for moral excellence alone will not make a success of life. Aristotle would not have agreed with the later Stoics, who held that interior moral virtue is sufficient and that we can be indifferent to external factors relating to our needs, our comforts, and our domestic and political circumstances. Nor would he have been in sympathy with the later views of Epicurus, who advocated detachment and withdrawal from the world as the prerequisite of happiness. As a social animal, man needs intercourse and communication with his fellows. There is a long section devoted to friendship, *philia*, in the *Ethics*. The Greek word for 'social' in this connection is *politikos*, for the good and happy life is only possible, in Aristotle's view, within society. The stateless man is either, like Homer's Cyclops, an ignoble savage, or a god (*Politics*, 1253a). In his view ethics and politics are virtually the same subject, the former concerning the good for man considered as an individual, the latter the good for man considered from the point of view of the state as a whole. The function of the state is not conquest, trade or empire, but to enable individuals to live the good life (*Politics*, 1252d). In particular it exists to provide the necessary leisure for the good life, for 'we occupy ourselves in order that we may have leisure, just as we make war for the sake of peace' (*Ethics*, X, 7). This leisure will be spent partly in relaxation and simple amusement, but the man who would be happy will use it to further the life of the intellect, for 'the intellect more than anything else is the man':

> intellectual activity, taking as it does the form of contempla-
> tion, seems to excel all other activities in the seriousness of its
> purpose, to aim at no end beyond itself and to have its own
> unique pleasure, which enhances its activity. In this activity
> we easily recognise self-sufficiency, the possibility of leisure
> and such freedom from fatigue as it is humanly possible,
> together with all the other blessings of pure happiness. . . . If
> the intellect is divine compared with man, the life of the
> intellect must be divine compared with the life of a human
> creature. And we ought not to listen to those who council us
> *O man, think as a man should* and *O mortal, remember your mortality.*
> Rather ought we, so far as in us lies, to put on immortality
> and to leave nothing unattempted in the effort to live in
> conformity with the highest thing within us.
>
> > (*Ethics*, **X**, 7)

Aristotelian philosophy, which emanates from the last years of the independent *polis* before the Macedonian conquest (and Aristotle had been criticised for showing no apparent awareness of the coming change), represents the final and in some senses the fullest philosophic expression of the best in classical Greek civilisation. The whole tendency of his thought, unlike that of Plato, works with and not against the grain of the best Athenian culture of his day. Here may be noted the purpose and value he sees in literature and art. Nevertheless, it must be admitted at once that there is a narrowness in his aristocratic outlook. He has not the respect of Herodotus for the non-Greek (*Politics*, 1252b). Slavery he considered entirely natural (*Politics*, 1254a). Unlike Plato, who advocates sexual equality in the *Republic*, he believes in the natural inferiority of women (*Politics*, 1252b). But in the range of his interests, he embraces more of life than Plato; no other Greek thinker opened up so many areas to intellectual enquiry. And his idea of the good life, less exclusive than that of the other-worldly Plato, comes from a generous affirmation of the purpose and value of earthly life. His own achievements provide the recommending context for his praise of the intellectual life.

POST-ARISTOTELIANS

With the passing of the city state, philosophy became less theoretical and more practical, offering the individual a design for living independent of external circumstances.

Zeno of Citium in Cyprus (*c.* 333–*c.* 262) was the founder of the Stoic School at Athens, so called from the Stoa Poikile, the colonnade, where Zeno and his successors, who included Cleanthes (*c.* 331–*c.* 213) and Chrysippus (*c.* 280–207), conducted their teaching. Zeno began philosophical life as one of the Cynics, whose chief doctrine was that self-sufficiency could bring contentment in all the vicissitudes of life. The most famous Cynic, Diogenes (*c.* 400–325), was reputed to have lived in a barrel in accordance with his belief that happiness consisted in satisfying only the most basic natural needs and in renouncing the world of conventional behaviour. The word cynic comes from his nickname, from *kyon-kynos*, dog, said to have been given to him for his shamelessness. From the austerities of cynicism, Zeno was converted by the writings of Antisthenes (*c.* 445–*c.* 360), a pupil and friend of Socrates (who may also have influenced

Figure 14   The Stoa of Attalus in Athens as reconstructed, *c.* 155

Diogenes), to Socratic philosophy whence he developed his own teaching, divided into three parts comprising logic, physics and ethics, the most enduring of which has been Stoic morality. Virtue is based upon knowledge; only the wise man can be truly virtuous and harmonise his reason with Nature which is ruled by the greater reason, the *Logos*, identified with god and manifested in fate. The wise man, ruled by reason, will be indifferent to the passions (apathetic) and independent of the vagaries of fortune (having self-rule, *autarcheia*) in the knowledge that pleasure is not a good, and pain and death are not evils. Cleanthes, Zeno's successor as head of the Stoic school, emphasises the religious side of the Stoic doctrine in his *Hymn to Zeus*.

> Most glorious and omnipotent Zeus, ruler of Nature, worshipped under many names, by whom all things are governed in accordance with Law, hail to thee! From thee we are born, and alone of all living things on the earth are created in the likeness of God. So I shall forever praise thy power, by which the heaven is moved and directed in its course around the earth, rejoicing in thy control. For thou hast as thy servant in thy victorious hands heaven's double-edged thunderbolt of imperishable fire, pulsing its way through every creature that obeys thee; and with it thou dost direct Universal Reason which moves through all creation, mingling with the sun and with the host of stars. All things on earth, in the sea, or in the air confess thee as their author, except the deeds of the evil and foolish; but even such discords thou knowest how to weave into a total harmony, making what is disorderly orderly, what is hostile friendly, in accordance with the Law of Reason which blind men cannot understand. Instead they suffer loss when they seek happiness in their own fashion, knowing not the Divine Law. Some of them pursue prestige, some wealth, some sensual delight. Fools they are, who strive in vain. But do thou, Zeus, giver of all, cloud-gatherer and lord of the lightning, save men from their bitter ignorance, dispel their sorrow and grief, and grant them wisdom, for by wisdom thou dost rule with power and justice. In return for thy blessing we give thee and thy work our everlasting praise. And there is no greater glory for men or for gods than to praise forever Universal Reason.

Later teachers adapted Stoic philosophy to Rome and it is through Roman rather than Greek writings that knowledge of Stoicism has come down to us, particularly through the works of Cicero (106–43), Seneca (4 BC–AD 65), Epictetus (AD 55–135) and Marcus Aurelius (AD 121–80).

Detachment from the world was a desideratum of the school of Epicurus (341–271), who settled in Athens in 307 where he bought a home with a garden, the latter giving its name, the Garden, to the philosophical school which he set up in it. Here he lived with his followers in ascetic seclusion. He identified pleasure (the absence of pain) with the good and aspired to *ataraxia*, freedom from disturbance. In one of his letters he is careful to distinguish the true pleasures of the Epicurean from those vulgarly attributed to his school.

> When we say, then, that pleasure is the end and aim, we do not mean the pleasures of the prodigal or the pleasures of sensuality, as we are understood to do by some through ignorance, prejudice, or wilful misrepresentation. By pleasure we mean the absence of pain in the body and of trouble in the soul. It is not an unbroken succession of drinking-bouts and of revelry, not sexual love, not the enjoyment of the fish and other delicacies of a luxurious table, which produces a pleasant life; it is sober reasoning, searching out the grounds of every choice and avoidance, and banishing those beliefs through which the greatest tumults take possession of the soul. Of all this the beginning and greatest good is prudence. Wherefore prudence is a more precious thing even than philosophy; from it springs all the other virtues, for it teaches that we cannot lead a life of pleasure which is not also a life of prudence, honour, and justice; nor lead a life of prudence, honour, and justice, which is not also a life of pleasure. For the virtues have grown into one with a pleasant life, and a pleasant life is inseparable from them.
>
> (Diogenes Laertius, *Life of Epicurus*, X, 131–2)

He took over the atomic theory of Democritus (460–*c*. 357), believing that the world came into existence by a chance collision of atoms. The gods exist, but they do so in serene detachment, taking no interest in humankind. There is no after-life, death being merely the dispersal of atoms in the individual and therefore no cause of fear. This he makes into a life-affirming doctrine.

> Accustom yourself to believe that death is nothing to us, for good and evil imply sentience, and death is the privation of all sentience; therefore, a right understanding that death is nothing to us makes the mortality of life enjoyable, not by adding to life an illimitable time, but by taking away the yearning for immortality. For life has no terrors for him who has thoroughly apprehended that there are no terrors for him in ceasing to live. . . . The wise man does not deprecate life nor does he fear the cessation of life. The thought of life is no offence to him, nor is the cessation of life regarded as an evil. And even as men choose of food not merely and simply the larger portion, but the more pleasant, so the wise seek to enjoy the time which is most pleasant and not merely that which is longest.
>
> (Diogenes Laertius, *Life of Epicurus*, X, 124–6)

His doctrines are the basis of the poem *On the Nature of Things* by the Roman Lucretius (98–55).

Advances were made in mathematics with the *Elements* of Euclid (*fl. c.* 300) and the discoveries of Archimedes (*c.* 287–212). Aristarchus of Samos even advanced the hypothesis of a heliocentric cosmology. As the Greeks did not invent the microscope or telescope, progress in experimental science was limited.

Greek philosophy has continued to be influential. Indeed, a modern thinker called all philosophy 'footnotes to Plato'. Plato's philosophy was given new expression in the Neoplatonism of the third century of the Christian era. Christian thinkers like Augustine (AD 354–430) owe much to this tradition. In the Middle Ages Aristotelian logic became the basis of scholasticism, while the Christian philosophy of Aquinas (AD 1225–74) was a fusion of Aristotelianism and theology.

5

ART

and generally art partly completes what nature cannot
bring to a finish, and partly imitates her.

Aristotle, *Physics*, II, 8 (199a 15)

POTTERY AND PAINTING

The art of the earliest Bronze Age civilisation on Crete and the
mainland (the Minoan and the Mycenaean) is of a high order, as
visitors to the remains of the royal palaces at Cnossos or the
great sites at Mycenae or Tiryns and to their accompanying
museums will testify. The fall of Mycenaean civilisation to
invading tribes from the west and the north (the so-called
Dorian invasion of the eleventh century) initiated a Dark Age
out of which gradually emerged the city state. The art of the city
state, despite some limited continuity with that of the displaced
culture, slowly took a new direction, developing the forms and
characteristics that are perfected in the art of the classical age.

Of the physical remains of Greek art that survive antiquity the
most substantial in all periods comprises the decorated pottery
that was used extensively in daily life and came to be traded
between states throughout the Greek world. It was manu-
factured in many centres and while the style of each centre
might vary, over the centuries definite stylistic phases can be
distinguished. The main periods and styles within which art
historians also distinguish various subdivisions are the geometric, which developed at Athens in the ninth and eight
centuries (these chronological divisions can only be roughly
made), the archaic in the seventh and sixth centuries, the
classical in the fifth and fourth, and the Hellenistic in the period

150

between the Macedonian conquest in the late fourth century and the Roman conquest in the mid-second century.

The geometric style

The geometric style, so called from the linear regularity of its ornamentation, represents an advance on the pottery of the preceding era (called the protogeometric) by virtue of the increased ornamentation covering the vase. A fine example of developed geometric is the magnificent Dipylon vase of about 750, so called from the place at which it was discovered in a cemetery by the Dipylon gate at Athens. The vase (fig. 15) is about 5 feet in height and stood as a monument over a grave. A prominent feature of the decoration is the meander or key pattern which is repeated (with variation) on the neck where it occurs three times and on the body where it is used four times in the horizontal bands as well as in vertical bands between the handles. There are rows of triangles and one row of oval shapes towards the bottom of the vase. The thick black bands painted at the top and the bottom of the neck, and the more extensive area of black at the base (together with the two thick bands there) accentuate the shape of the vessel, which is simply but finely proportioned.

On the neck are two bands of animal figures, all in the same attitude; in the upper band they are grazing while in the lower they are lying down. The animal figures are made to fit easily into the pattern of abstract designs. Between the handles, in a central position to which the eye is unerringly drawn, is framed a representation of mourners at a funeral, a subject which reflects the purpose of the pot. The human figures have the form that predominates in early Greek painting, with a triangular chest tapering to a thin waist and highly developed thighs in a roughly ovular tear drop shape tapering to the knee. The chest is full frontal while the legs and head are in profile. The arms above the head in mourning attitude complete a triangle which ascends from the waist. The same pattern is repeated for the corpse, which consequently appears to be suspended in mid-air above the bier.

The vase is a highly sophisticated work of art but the painting of the human figures is naive; the parts of the body are simply stylised shapes that do not correspond to the natural shape of the

Figure 15   The Dipylon vase (Athens: National Museum)

human form. Moreover, the proportions of the figures in relation to each other are not determined by nature. The size of the figures below the corpse matches neither the size of the standing mourners nor the corpse. Similarly, the corpse is longer than the standing figures are tall. Their proportions are designed to satisfy geometrical considerations, for the composition of the human scene is split into four parts which have a broadly symmetrical relation but interestingly there is a little variation in that on the left-hand side of the bier there are seven mourners while on the right there are six and a tiny figure like that of a child. The central scene is divided horizontally between the corpse at the top and the mourners at the bottom, two of which are kneeling while the others are sitting, varying the symmetry.

The representation of human figures is regarded by art historians as a breakthrough because the geometric style had been fully abstract. This must explain the small area of space given to the central image of the mourning scene (in which the corpse is centrally situated and dominates by virtue of size) when considered in relation to the whole surface area of the vase. Despite this, the human scene *is* nevertheless curiously central, for the eye is drawn to it not only for the principal reason that it is situated between the handles at the broadest point of the pot. For the vertical black figures contrast with the predominantly horizontal patterned bands of the rest of the vase, while the horizontal black line of the corpse corresponds to them. The band enclosing the human scene is broader than any of the geometrically patterned bands of the body of the pot and has a larger area of pale background colour which intensifies the black figures. There is a similar effect of colour in the band of animals in the neck of the pot with a lighter background highlighting the black shapes. Furthermore, the two animal bands offset the more prominent human scene.

The design is therefore more complex than it might at first seem, since it looks deceptively simple. It is a balance of repetition and variation (and there are variations within the repetitions), designed to highlight the human scene through the subtle use of proportion, shape and colour. The component geometric parts can be said to cohere in a unified whole which expresses the function for which it is designed.

Archaic black-figure style

Not long after the date of the Dipylon vase, in about 720, at Corinth a new and freer style developed following oriental models and introducing animal and plant motifs. The use of plants in decoration continued to classical times, though interest in animals diminished in favour of an emphasis upon the human, whether in the depiction of mythological figures or in scenes from everyday life.

The Corinthian jug (fig. 16) dated about 630, is a fine example of this style in its maturity. Three prominent bands divide the pot into sections as in the geometric style, but the intervening designs are what interest the artist. The winged mythical creature, reminiscent of the Egyptian sphinx, with her roughly triangular shape fits in well with the tapering contours of the top of the vase. The flourish of the wing and the tail offset the statuesque dignity of the shapely human head and hair. The artist has taken care with the detail of the figures: the headband on the hair, the feathers on the wing, the claws and sinews of the limbs. The bulky forms of the larger-bodied creatures amply fill the central band and add solidity to the overall design of the jug. The animals are recognisable (boars and perhaps a mastiff dog) but are clearly stylised, looking rather like silhouettes. Once again there is detail in the representation of the faces, the ribs and paws of the dog, and the sinews and hooves of the boars. The lower section, with its airy movement and slender creatures (greyhounds and a hare), reflects the more feathery delicacy of the top panel. But there is no strong correspondence between the parts of the whole as in the geometrical style. The animals do not face the same way and the flowers simply fill in the spaces. There is no discernible pattern in the decoration. There is a unifying element in the dual-tone colouring of the animals, but again the colouring is used differently in each individual creature. Working within the clear boundaries made by the horizontal bands, the artist seeks a free representation of his subject.

Pottery of the archaic period reaches its culmination at Athens in the mid-sixth century. A beautiful example of the finest archaic style is the vase depicting Achilles and Ajax playing draughts (the protagonists are named on the vase), executed and signed by the Athenian Exekias *c.* 530 (fig. 17). The heroes

Figure 16 Corinthian jug, *c.* 630 (Munich: Antikensammlung)

ART

Figure 17 Vase of Exekias (Rome: Vatican)

156

are so rapt in concentration that they do not hear the call to battle.

The vase has been beautifully conceived as a whole. The plain black areas of the neck and the lower half offset the central band encompassing the painting. The light background of the handles links well with the light background on which the figures are painted. A more subtle link is provided by the pale band at the base broken by a dark upward pointing spearhead motif. The design of the painting itself is simple and clear and beautifully proportioned to the contours and shape of the vase. The curves of the bending heroes' backs reflect the curves of the vase, as do the diminishing rectangles of the seats, which are almost curved when compared to the central square on which the game is being played. From the baseline on either side, the curve of the foreshortened shield is carried to the base of the handle, continues through the handle to be picked up by the point of the spears, whence it is carried to the focal point of the square upon which all the attention is concentrated. The square is perfectly situated in relation to the vase as a whole.

The two figures are almost mirror images of each other in their posture, costume and armour, but the artist has avoided the rigidity of too symmetrical a scheme. First, the two sets of spears form a central triangle within which are framed the two heads and the playing hands, the focus of concentration, and this central triangle gives the composition a tripartite structure rather than an exact bipartite symmetry. Although it is possible to see a geometric pattern, the lines of it are not rigid and the elements are sufficiently varied to impart naturalism.

The two spears of the helmeted figure (Achilles) cross and so seem to be slightly curved softening the straight lines and giving a lifelike touch. The two sets of spears meet at an imaginary point off-centre, not immediately below the playing hands and just below the focal point. The most obvious asymmetrical feature is in the position of the two helmets. It is not only that Achilles is wearing his while Ajax is not, but also that the curving lines of the helmet and plume (reflecting the curves of the vase's handles) depart from the symmetry by both facing the same way. One effect of the helmet on the head is to enhance the stature and status of Achilles. But with both heroes wearing their helmets the composition would have been radically different. As it is, the helmet on the head makes a canopy of curves above the game board and the curving plume is directly central. The effect is to unify the composition by linking the top of the picture to the square at the bottom. At the same time the helmet breaks the symmetry within the central triangle and also punctures the precision of the semicircle made by the two bowed figures. Also, the 'eye' of the helmet acts as a third eye; it reflects the eye of Achilles, and the imaginary line of its vision is directed towards the head of Ajax. The third eye therefore functions as a link between the two heroes while breaking the symmetry. The position of the helmet also enables the artist to unify the sweep of the figure in a series of downward-pointing lines from the pointed end of the plume, the noseguard and the end of the helmet itself, and the corresponding nose and beard of Achilles, and also the pointed end of his cloak near the shoulders right down to the pointed ends of his cloak overlapping the seat. The knee guard pointing upwards acts as a counterpoint to this series. The much praised harmony of this vase is achieved by a masterly ordering of the parts. The geometrical symmetry is enhanced and enlivened by subtle variation.

Further examination of the detail of the design shows that the figures, although broadly similar in form, are clearly differentiated. As befits his superior status as the supreme Greek warrior, Achilles not only wears his helmet but is slightly larger in his dimensions. The artist has also included more detail in the execution of his figure; his hand and feet are more delicately drawn. Moreover, his playing hand is framed between the lines of the two spears. His costume is more detailed and the design of the shield more prominent. There are subtle differences between the two heads. Ajax has curly hair and a rugged beard while Achilles' hair is smoother and his beard more trim. The refinement of details is fully functional in giving Achilles his superior status.

The artist includes animal and floral motifs (on the shield and on the cloaks), but these are subordinate to the human figures. The vase is highly detailed, but all the details reflect a central purpose and there is no superfluous decoration. The artistic concentration perfectly matches the theme of the painting.

Red-figure innovation

The figures of the Exekian vase are painted in black silhouette upon the red clay of the pot. The potter then used an engraving tool as an incisor to give detailed lines to his form. A major technical innovation occurred in the generation following Exekias when an Athenian potter in about 530 reversed the process by painting an outline of his figures and then colouring the background black so that the figures remained red. The drawing of the figures was then completed not with an engraving tool but with a brush whose supple strokes could be more readily varied to give fluidity and depth to the figures. The subsequent red-figure technique gradually made the old method of black-figure painting redundant. Painters took advantage of the flexible technique of drawing to represent human anatomy and expression more naturally.

Wonderful as it is, Exekias' representation of the heroic warriors seems stiff and formal when set beside the girl going to wash on an Athenian cup (fig. 18) painted in the early fifth century, little more than a generation later. In the overall design there is still some trace of geometric patterning. The girl's head, the pail and the basin form a basic triangular frame within which there are two other lop-sided triangles formed by the head, the bundle of clothes and the pail, and by the pail, the bundle and the basin. The composition, reflecting the shape it is filling – note the incline of the head, the backward stretch of the arm and the curve of the back foot – is roughly circular. The handle of the pail and the handle of the basin provide a link across the painting. Furthermore, there is a predilection for rounded forms, in the bundle, in the pail, in the various curves of the figure (particularly the buttocks), and in the curvaceous basin. But the overall patterning is less marked and more difficult to describe than the design of Exekias. What is immediately striking is the relaxed naturalism of this arrested moment as the girl moves towards the basin. Although the head is in profile, its incline, together with the corresponding alignment of the shoulder, the gentle twisting of the torso and the slightly raised back leg together give the impression of a moving figure at a pivotal moment. (The archaic convention that figures should be strictly frontal or profile, or a combination of the two to represent the body in motion, has been broken.) The beauty of this slightly androgynous figure stems from the delicately executed artistry of the pose. On reflection, it can be see that it would be extremely difficult to attain this pose in actuality: the arm extended backwards carrying a large pail would create

Figure 18 Athenian cup: girl going to wash (Brussels: Musée des Beaux Arts)

great strain; in fact, the pail would naturally be held much closer to the body. So while the stiffness of the archaic style has been softened and its two-dimensional quality opened up, the new experimental style is only partially naturalistic. Elements of stylisation continue to exist in the hair and in the lines of the drapery in the girl's hand, and the artistry of the pose is more obvious in its arrangement than will be the case in the later classical style.

At the beginning of the classical period in the 470s, further innovations took place as vase painters experimented with techniques initiated by one of the early masters of classical picture painting, Polygnotus. None of his works survives but from descriptions of them in later writers art historians have attributed to him a key role in the revolution whereby painting become three-dimensional with limited use of perspective to create the illusion of space. For the first time in the fifth century, vase painters created scenes in which figures were not all placed on the same baseline.

The Niobid-painter (so called from the subject of the scene on the reverse side of the vase in figure 19 featuring the killing of the children of Niobe) has a group of figures deliberately spaced at different levels, though since he has not recessed any of them by making them smaller, they seem to be floating in space. This is especially true of the figure to the right of the centre clasping his leg, who appears to be sitting in mid-air with his lower foot rather awkwardly resting on the knee of the reclining figure.

The subject of this side of the vase (fig. 19) is uncertain. It has sometimes been thought to represent the Argonauts. The warriors are evidently in a relaxed mood. Though the two shields and the circular decoration at the bottom left together make a triangle, and the three sharp lines of the spears link figures and give overall form to the composition, there is not the rigorously conceived geometric structure that had been the basis from which Exekias perfected his art. The foreshortening of the two shields is not designed, as in the painting of Exekias, to blend in with the contours of the vase but is clearly a naturalistic effect for its own sake to create the illusion of depth. The composition of the Niobid-painter, which lacks the concentration of a single focal point, is more relaxed and casual as reflected in his chosen theme.

The relaxed poses of the four central figures are all quite

Figure 19 Niobid vase (Paris: Louvre)

different. The helmeted and costumed figure at the top left in three-quarters view rests with his knee against his shield. The full-frontal nude figure with a garland on his head stands at ease with his weight on his right foot posed like a classical statue except that his head is in sharp profile. The reclining figure at the bottom elegantly supports himself with one arm on the ground and one on his spears. The fourth figure clasping his leg is in a sitting position even though he does not appear to have a seat.

162

The figure with the fine three-quarters face is perhaps the most ambitious and also the least successful. To create a relaxed naturalistic pose the painter has experimented with the length of the limbs, but the front leg and the far arm seem too long, and the near shoulder seems bent. In the representation of the human form, painting has now freed itself from the conventions of archaic art, whereby the chest tapers to a thin waist and the ovular thighs are unduly developed, and has adopted instead the new anatomical structure of recent sculpture where the centre of the body is filled out (see p. 182). The lines of the muscular thorax of the standing nude are perhaps a little schematic, but the more fluid lines of the reclining figure impart grace and ease without diminishing the warrior's strength. The reclining figure successfully combines the formality of the standing nude with the relaxed naturalism of the sitting figure.

This beautiful red-figure vase does not have the perfection achieved in the black-figure style of Exekias, but the painter is experimenting and working in a new and freer style. On vases from this time onwards, foreshortening, particularly of objects like pedestals, shields or buildings, becomes commonplace, but experiments with spatial effects like that of the Niobid-painter were soon abandoned. Perhaps it seemed a perverse breach of decorum to attempt a deepening perspective whereby the painted scene works against the natural contours of the vase by seeming to penetrate the pot. Painters working on the flat surface of a wall might feel less inhibited.

Classical painting

In the absence of any surviving originals, the history of Greek painting has to be inferred from later copies (sometimes in the form of mosaics) and has to be reconstructed from accounts of it in later writings, particularly those of the elder Pliny (AD 23/4–79), a Roman polymath who has a long section on Greek art in his *Natural History.* Apollodorus, an Athenian painter of the mid- to late fifth century, was nick-named 'the shadow painter', which suggests that he was the first to make extensive use of high-lighting by means of shading, a technique scarcely used in the line drawing of the vase painters. Pliny says he was the first to give a realistic presentation of objects and that he paved the way for his younger contemporary Zeuxis of Heraclea (*Natural History,*

XXXV, 60). Pliny also records a trial of skill between Zeuxis and
Parrhasius of Ephesus in the art of illusion. Zeuxis produced a
picture of grapes so successfully represented that birds flew up to
the stage building where the paintings were exhibited. Parrhasius' contribution was a picture of a curtain so naturalistic that
Zeuxis mistakenly asked for it to be drawn aside, thinking that
Parrhasius' painting was behind it (XXXV, 65). The anecdote
suggests absolute mastery of shading, foreshortening and mixing
of colour in the interests of naturalistic illusion. (Whether the
Greeks composed painting with fully developed perspective,
having a single vanishing point, has been much debated.)

However, the Greek artist did not aim simply to copy nature,
as Socrates suggests in a conversation with Parrhasius recorded
in Xenophon's *Memoirs of Socrates*:

> When you are painting beautiful figures, as it isn't easy to
> come across one single model who is beyond criticism in
> every detail, you combine the best feature of each one of a
> number of models, and so convey the appearance of entirely
> beautiful bodies.
>
> (III, 10, 2)

According to the Roman writer Cicero (106–43), this was the
method of Zeuxis. When commissioned by the people of Croton
to decorate their temple of Hera, he desired to paint a picture of
Helen of Troy which might embody the perfection of female
beauty. From the young women assembled by the citizenry he
chose the five most beautiful 'because he did not think that all
the qualities which he sought to combine in a portrayal of beauty
could be found in one person, because in no case has Nature
made anything perfect and finished in every part' (*On Invention*,
II, 3). The resulting image (which does not of course survive)
could be said to be typical, meaning not that she constituted an
average norm but rather the ideal of the type, for Zeuxis added
to his painting the words of Homer uttered by the old men of
Troy: 'who on earth could blame the Trojan and Achaean men
at arms for suffering so long for such a woman's sake? Indeed she
is the very image of an immortal goddess' (*Iliad*, III, 156–8).

The theory and practice of Parrhasius and Zeuxis suggest the
context for interpreting what Aristotle means when he says that
art imitates nature, and art carries things further than nature
(*Physics*, II, 8, 15). Like nature, the artist imposes form (*eidos*)

upon the undifferentiated matter of the world (*hyle*), but the artist can also transcend nature by ironing out her imperfections. In eschewing the abnormal and the eccentric, the classical artist concentrates upon the essence and works through the particular and the individual to express the typical and the ideal.

Vase painting, by dint of limitations both inherent and self-imposed, does not represent the pinnacle of Greek achievement in painting, which came later than in other areas of art with Apelles of Cos, who was a court artist of Alexander in the late fourth century and acknowledged to be the greatest painter of antiquity. Nevertheless, the art of line drawing in the free Attic style of the age of Pericles in the mid-fifth century has rarely been surpassed. A master of the art is the Achilles-painter, so called from his most famous vase depicting Achilles and Briseis, to whom are also attributed a number of white ground funeral vases called *lekythoi* (oil flasks).

The *lekythos* illustrated (fig. 20) depicts a girl playing a lyre. The Greek word at the bottom right, Helicon, the seat of the Muses, indicates that she herself might be one of the nine. The musical motif is continued in the presence of the bird at the girl's feet. The composition and drawing are extremely simple; the ground and the seat are indicated by single lines, the curves of which are parallel to the curving lines of the main figure upon which all the attention is concentrated. More detail on the seat or the ground would have detracted from this concentration. The Achilles-painter has anticipated the virtue of artistic tact upon which, according to Pliny, the master Apelles prided himself when he said that 'he knew when to take his hand away from a picture' (*Natural History*, XXXV, 80).

The Muse is gazing into the middle distance and the very slight curve to her lips might indicate pleasure. She may easily be imagined to be serenely contemplating the beautiful sound of the music she is making, for this is the mood that the painter has successfully imparted to the painting.

Its simple harmony may seem to defy analysis, but on reflection much of its satisfying sense of completeness stems from the beautiful sense of proportion in the broad outlines of the design, imparting to the whole a pleasing unity. The sweeping curves of the back, the thighs and the legs make a sequence in which the three major elements are perfectly proportioned. Into the central sweep of the main curve from neck to knee fits the smaller

Figure 20   Lekythos by the Achilles-painter (Munich: Antikensammlung:
von Schoen Collection)

and sharper curve of the lyre. The main curve is counterba-
lanced both by the vertical line of the drapery (tapering into a
corresponding curve), which is directly below the head and neck
(thus reinforcing the painting's gravitational centre), and by the

arm and a series of straight lines including the fingers and the strings and frame of the lyre, all bisecting the curves at an angle of roughly 45 degrees. This series itself is crossed almost at right angles by the white band and top string of the lyre. If the line of the headband, the line of the arm from the elbow to the forefinger and the line of the legs were to be continued left-wards, they would all meet at the edge of the vase, so that they may be said to form a series of radial lines on the main semicircular curve. Of course, the beauty of the painting does not simply arise from the design with its approximation to geometric patterns – such patterning could equally result in stiffness and artificiality – but their presence underlying the apparent naturalism of the surface must contribute to the beauty of its proportions and perhaps suggest that at its best Greek art, even in its maturity, never entirely lost contact with its geometrical origins.

The final masterly touch in the overall design may be seen in the positioning of the bird. Its body forms a parallel line with the arm and the straight lines bisecting the main curve of the girl's body. Together with the headband it is almost an edging frame to the whole structure, while the ground line on which it is situated continues and completes the main curving sequence that begins with the incline of the head and flows through the body in a most satisfying way. We need only imagine the bird facing the other way, or at the other side of the figure or on a level with her toes, to appreciate the appropriateness of its positioning in the overall design.

The beauty of the painting stems also from its fluidity and refinement. The slight incline of the head and the tapering line of the feet give the whole structure a delicate poise. There is refinement too in the execution of detail, in the curls of the hair and in the different textures of the headband, the smooth material of the chiton above and below the darker rumpled material of the outer dress, and even in the suggestion of feathers in the figure of the bird. None of the detail is fussy or draws attention to itself; everything has its place in the larger design.

Despite the apparent naturalism there is an element of style most obviously in the 'Grecian profile' in which the forehead and nose are united in a continuous straight line, and perhaps also in the 'Grecian bend' of the slightly rounded shoulders. The

Grecian attitude is clearly ideal but the style of the pose is not exaggerated to the point where it becomes affected or mannered. In this restraint of style classical art is to be distinguished from the greater stylistic extravagance of mannerism or the baroque. In the clarity and economy of its general outline, in the unity of its design where the parts are subordinate to the whole in a harmoniously proportioned structure, in the natural ease of its fluent style with its tendency to ideal expression and in the restrained decorum of its content and form where there is nothing in excess, the beautiful and dignified music of the Achilles-painter may be regarded as a touchstone distinguishing the calm, the poise and the uplifting serenity of classical art.

ARCHITECTURE

These qualities are also embodied in the architectural achievements of the Greeks, the finest of which is the Parthenon, the temple dedicated to the presiding goddess of the city, Athene Parthenos (meaning 'maiden'), dramatically situated on the Athenian Acropolis, the top point of the city. At the outset of his history of the Peloponnesian War, Thucydides speculates as to the effect on posterity of the public buildings of the two great rival powers of Sparta and Athens:

> Suppose, for example, that the city of Sparta were to become deserted and that only the temples and foundations of buildings remained, I think that future generations would, as time passed, find it very difficult to believe that this place had really been as powerful as it was represented to be. Yet the Spartans occupy two-fifths of the Peloponnese and stand at the head not only of the whole Peloponnese itself but also of numerous allies beyond its frontiers. Since, however, the city is not regularly planned and contains no temples or monuments of great magnificence, but is simply a collection of villages, in the ancient Hellenic way, its appearance would not come up to expectation. If, on the other hand, the same thing were to happen to Athens, one would conjecture from what met the eye that the city had been twice as powerful as in fact it is.
>
> (I, 10)

His words were of course prophetic. The Parthenon, even in its ruined state, has become an inspiring symbol of Athenian great-

Figure 21 Model restoration of the Athenian Acropolis with the Propylaea and the temple of Athene Nike (completed in 424) in the right foreground, the Parthenon (completed in 432) beyond and the Erechtheum (completed in 406) to the left centre (Royal Ontario Museum, Toronto)

ness and of the spirit that distinguished the Athenian from the Spartan, a symbol of the Athenian cultivation of the Greek feeling for beauty that the Spartans had repressed. (There are no Spartan remains to stir the imagination.) More than a symbol, it is a real cultural emblem, the marble embodiment of the classical spirit (fig. 21).

The motive force behind its building is suggested by the later Greek historian Plutarch (AD *c*. 50–120) in his *Life of Pericles*:

> When the Spartans began to be vexed by the growing power of Athens, Pericles, by way of encouraging the people to cherish ever higher ambitions and making them believe themselves capable of great achievements, introduced a proposal that all the Greeks . . . should be invited to send delegates to a congress at Athens. The subjects to be discussed were the Greek sanctuaries which had been burned down by the Persians . . . and the security of the seas.
>
> (17)

The Spartans would have nothing to do with the plan, so the Panhellenic congress never took place. But Pericles went ahead with the restoration of the temples on the Acropolis that the invading Persians had destroyed, and the Parthenon was begun in 447, to be finally completed fifteen years later. We may say that the motive was political in the sense that the grand vision of Pericles was designed to express and enhance the growing confidence and self-awareness of the Athenian *polis*.

Plutarch vividly describes the energy that went into the new construction:

> So the buildings arose, as imposing in their sheer size as they were inimitable in the grace of their outlines, since the artists strove to excel themselves in the beauty of their workmanship. And yet the most wonderful thing about them was the speed with which they were completed. Each of them, men supposed, would take many generations to build, but in fact the entire project was carried through in the high summer of one man's administration.
>
> (13)

Three years after the completion of the Parthenon, in his funeral oration over the Athenian dead, Thucydides has Pericles give voice to the Athenian cultural ideal: 'Our love of what is beautiful does not lead to extravagance; our love of things of the mind does not make us soft' (II, 40). The Greek phrase, which is literally rendered as 'with economy' and often put into its converse form 'without extravagance', is not to be understood as referring to cost, for no expense was spared in the project, for which funds were diverted from the treasury (made up of contributions from the allies). Beauty with economy and without extravagance is an aesthetic ideal perfectly embodied in the classical art of the Periclean age.

The design of the temple, the main form of Greek architecture, is well established as early as the seventh century. The roots of classical architecture go back to the ancient Egyptian, Minoan and Mycenaean civilisations. The Egyptians used columns to decorate their temples and tombs, and the Minoans used the method of construction known as 'trabeation', that is the placing of horizontal beams or lintels across the top of load-bearing upright posts or columns to form the 'entablature'. In the development of Greek architecture, there are two main stylistic orders (the Greek word for column is *stylos*), the Doric that had evolved as the predominant form on mainland Greece, and the Ionic which developed in Ionia and the Aegean islands in the late sixth century. The Doric is the more severe and grand; the Ionic, with its taller and thinner columns and its greater decoration, is the more graceful (see fig. 22b). The later Corinthian order, which was the predominant form of temple architecture in imperial Rome, is a variation of the Ionic with a distinctive capital (see fig. 22c). The Parthenon is regarded as the perfection of the Doric order.

Religious ceremonies were performed at an altar in the open air. The function of the temple was to house the cult statue of the presiding deity and to act as a storeroom for the deity's property. The greater size of the Parthenon (having eight columns at the front rather than the usual six and seventeen columns at the side, at least two more than usual) may have been connected with the enormous size of the cult statue of Athene, some 40 feet high, executed by the greatest sculpture of the age, Pheidias. The architects of the Parthenon, Ictinus and Callicrates, must have worked in conjunction with Pheidias, and Plutarch records that the latter, who was a friend of Pericles, had a general supervisory role over the whole project.

The basic rectilinear pattern was subjected by the architects to numerous refinements, to please the eye and possibly to correct optical illusions. The tapering columns of a Greek temple draw the eye upwards from the base to the roof, providing a natural link from top to bottom. On the Parthenon, more subtly than on other temples, the columns are not only tapered but are also given a slight inward curve. The architrave is given a slight outward or upward curve and the platform from which the temple rises is slightly convex. Such modifications in perspective soften the stark angularity of the basic geometric structure and give the temple a more natural relation to the ground on which it is built. The subtlety of the developed Greek style may be appreciated in a comparison of the photograph of the Parthenon (fig. 23a) with that of the earlier temple of Poseidon at Paestum (fig. 23b), more often referred to as the temple of Neptune, the Roman name of the god). The Parthenon is actually the larger structure (with more columns), yet its proportions are such as to endow it with a grandeur that is refined with a new grace when compared with the stockier (but nevertheless imposing)

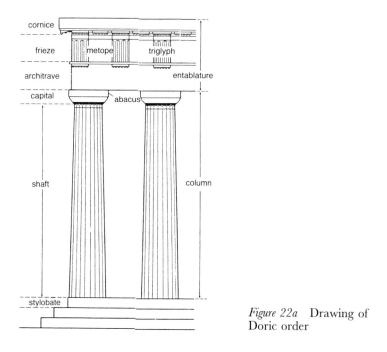

Figure 22a Drawing of Doric order

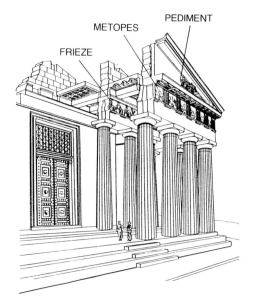

Figure 22d
Sectional
drawing of the
reconstructed
Parthenon

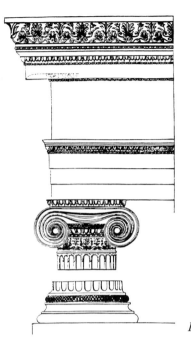

Figure 22b   Drawing of Ionic order

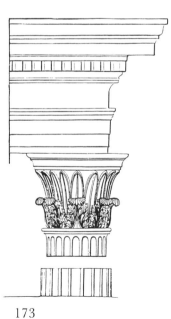

Figure 22c   Drawing of a
Corinthian capital

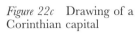

Figure 23a   The Parthenon (*photograph: Richard Stoneman*)

Figure 23b   Photograph of the temple of Poseidon

structures of the earlier part of the fifth century. The beauty of Greek architecture may be further appreciated if the temples are compared with the massive and solid structures of the Egyptians or with the static cubes and lifeless surfaces of much modern architecture.

There is considerable decoration on Greek architecture, but the decoration is not allowed to interrupt, as it often does in the Gothic style, the dominant lines of the structure as a whole. The parts are subordinate and not allowed to detract from the overall unity. Sculptural decoration of the building is confined, according to the Doric canon, to three areas, the triangular pediments at either end, the inner frieze and the metopes (see fig. 22d). Other surfaces of the fluted columns, the architraves and the exterior walls of the inner building known as the *cella*, are plain. The Parthenon differs from other Doric temples in the ambitious extent of its decoration, in that all the metopes and the whole of the inner frieze (covering a very large area) are sculpted. The marble (obtained locally from Mount Pentelikon) was then painted. The colour scheme of course no longer survives, but the effect of the colour on the buildings and the sculptures must have made the originals dramatically different from the most complete part of the ruined remains.

Apart from the ravages of time, the building suffered two particular disasters. The first occurred when it was converted into a Christian church in the fifth or sixth century of the Christian era, resulting in the loss of the centre of the east pediment. After the Turkish conquest of Greece in the fifteenth century AD it became a mosque, but the second and greatest disaster occurred in AD 1687 when it was used as an arsenal by the Turks in their war with the Venetians and a large part of the centre of the building was blown out.

Despite its incomplete state, much of the design of the original sculptures can be reconstructed. A late Greek writer, Pausanias, who wrote a *Description of Greece* in the second century AD when the building was still intact, records that the pediment above the entrance represented the birth of Athene, while the other showed a contest between Athene and Poseidon, god of the sea, for the land of Attica. Drawings by a visiting artist made before AD 1687 help to complete the picture of the pediments, the sculptures of which were carved completely in the round

175

ART

with reclining figures at the narrow end, then seated figures ascending to the principal standing figures at the centre.

Many of the individual metopes, carved in relief, survive. The main subjects appear to have been the battle between the gods and the giants on the east side, the battle between the Greeks and the Amazons (female warriors) on the west, the battle between the Lapiths and Centaurs (creatures who were half man and half horse) on the south, with scenes from the sack of Troy on the north. None of these subjects has any special connection with Athene, and these dramatic battle scenes, which were also popular on other temples, evidently gave the craftsmen maximum scope in the exercise of their art. It has also been argued that in the decorative sculptures as a whole there are the recurrent themes of the triumph of reason over chaos and of Hellenism over barbarism.

The subject of the inner frieze, where the upper part of the sculptures were carved in higher relief to allow for the steep angle of view, is not from traditional myth, and in this departure is an innovation. The frieze is wholly devoted to a representation of the Panathenaic procession, the annual festival held in honour of Athene in late summer. Every four years came the Great Panathenaea, when the object of the even more splendid ceremonial procession was to provide a new robe or *peplos* for the goddess. At a climactic point on the eastern frieze over the main door the *peplos* is presented to a magistrate while the spectacle is watched by the Olympian gods including Athene herself.

Only a little of the sculpture remains on the temple itself. In AD 1799 Lord Elgin, the British ambassador to Turkey (still in control of Greece), alarmed at the deteriorating condition of the sculptures, obtained permission to remove a substantial portion of the remains to London for safer keeping, where they can now be seen in the British Museum.

SCULPTURE

The sculptures of the Parthenon were completed in the high classical period, of which they are the chief surviving representatives. In sculpture, more clearly than in painting or architecture, it is possible to trace the gradual evolution whereby Greek art transcended the early formalism of the archaic period to become more naturalistic while remaining ideal, until the

176

emphasis upon the ideal and the typical in classical art gave way to individuality and realism in the art of the Hellenistic age.

Archaic beginnings

The earliest Greek statues seem to have been sculpted according to the Egyptian model. The *kouros* (young man) found in Attica (fig. 24a) and dating from 620 to 610 has the look of the Pharoahs especially noticeable in the stylisation of the hair and in the pose whereby one leg is planted firmly in front of the other. The rigidity of the stance, with the weight distributed equally between both legs, the arms fixed to the thighs with clenched hands, the shoulders absolutely square and the head directly frontal, is also part of the Egyptian tradition. But there are three respects in which the Greek differs from the Egyptian.

In the first place, the figure is completely nude where the Egyptian statues are either wholly costumed or discreetly draped about the loins. Nudity is singled out by Thucydides as a mark of progress that distinguishes the modern from the old-fashioned and the Greek from the non-Greek:

[The Spartans], too, were the first to play games naked, to take off their clothes openly, and to rub themselves down with olive oil after their exercise. In ancient times even at the Olympic Games the athletics used to wear coverings for their loins, and indeed this practice was still in exercise not many years ago. Indeed one could point to a number of other instances where the manners of the ancient Hellenic world are very similar to the manners of foreigners today.

(I, 6)

The Spartans even went so far as to have women exercising almost naked. In this they were exceptional. The Athenians were more restricted about female nakedness and their statues of young women were correspondingly draped. It was not until the fourth century that the first female nude appears and then the pose is modest (fig. 36). There must be some connection between the acceptance of male nudity in the actual life of the athlete in the gymnasium (from the Greek word *gymnos* which means 'naked') and the development of the male nude as the favoured form of Greek sculpture, whether as young man (*kouros*) or young god (Apollo).

177

Figure 24a   Archaic *kouros* (New York: Metropolitan Museum of Art)

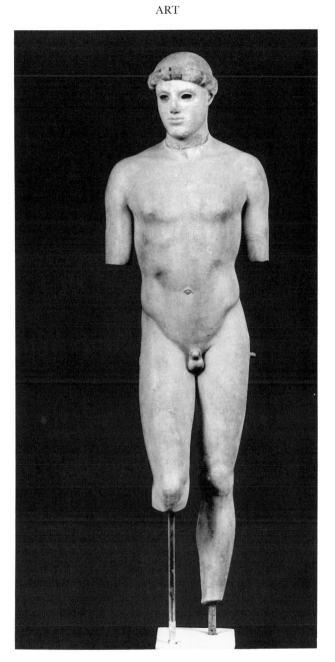

Figure 24b   Critian boy (Athens: Acropolis Museum)

Second, whereas the Egyptian figures are supported from the back or given some prop from the stone block out of which they are carved, the Greek figure is autonomous and free-standing. In comparison with later Greek statues, of course, the archaic *kouros* seems stiff and rigid, but in comparison with the immobile Egyptian, there is more articulation in the body and more than a hint of the potential movement that will be actualised in the freer and more flexible forms of the future.

Third, while the Egyptian statues seem to have been designed to show likeness of particular individuals (and certainly there are individual features in the faces), the Greek *kouros* is typical and ideal, without any attempt to render individuality. Both the face and the body are sculpted with geometric patterns in mind. Most noticeable are the corresponding triangles above and below the waist with the navel at the centre. There are recessed triangles in the elbows too. The pectoral muscles form an elegant double semicircle that can be seen to be repeated above the knees. The most striking feature of the face (apart from the round frame of the stylised hair) is the large eyes, the upper lids of which are semicircular. The semicircle is repeated in the line of the eyebrows. The Greek is therefore more abstract than individual, though if we compare the statue with the more rudimentary abstract figures of the Dipylon vase (fig. 15), the abstractions bear a closer relation to the actual and the natural. In the archaic *kouros* can be seen a characteristic preoccupation with proportion and symmetry underlying the Greek quest for ideal beauty.

The *kouros* discovered by archaeologists excavating the Athenian Acropolis in the late nineteenth century represents a remarkable advance (fig. 24b). It must have been made before the Persians destroyed the temples in 480, and is traditionally attributed to one of the leading sculptors of the period, Critios. The stiffness and rigid symmetries of the archaic style have been relaxed in the new pose, in which the weight is shifted on to the back leg with the hips raised accordingly. Although the arms are incomplete, the presence of small joints on the body makes it clear that they were fixed to the thighs as before, but the left upper arm is bent backwards slightly, suggesting that the arm was bent at the elbow, while the right arm drops vertically. Legs and arms are asymmetrically balanced. The slight turn of the head further softens the rigidity of the old pose, while the

Figure 25   Olympian Apollo (Olympia Museum)

recessed eyes are more lifelike, and the shortening of the hair not only gives greater clarity to the outlines of the head, but diminishes the effect of stylisation that is a marked feature of the archaic long-haired *kouros*. The centre of the torso has been filled out and its contours are gently curved. Suddenly the stone has been given a natural life.

Three further examples from the earlier classical period illustrate different aspects of its achievement. The sublime head of Apollo (fig. 25) from the pediment of the temple of Zeus at Olympia (*c.* 460) has a godlike beauty, authority and power. The standing god, whose body has a straight frontal pose, is situated at the central point of the pediment, the subject of which is the battle of the Lapiths and Centaurs. One of his arms is outstretched and his head, though not in profile, is turned and looking towards the battling figures. The calm majesty of the god, who can be imagined to be ordering or rebuking the bestial Centaurs, contrasts with the chaotic movement of the inferior beings. The imperiousness of the facial attitude complements the statuesque severity of the body. The noble face is strongly supported by the neck and crowned by the clear moulding of the hair with its orderly locks following the curve of the temples and forehead and framing it to its best advantage. The features of the face – the straight nose, the large eyes with fine eyebrows, the beautifully formed lips, the strong chin and cheekbones, and the flawless complexion present an unforgettable image of ideal male beauty.

Equally sublime and assured, but this time representing a more dynamic pose, is the mighty bronze statue of a god, usually identified as Poseidon but sometimes as Zeus, discovered in the sea off the coast of cape Artemisium (fig. 27). The god is thought to be about to hurl the trident (or thunderbolt) and is an image of concentrated energy and power. The face, gesticulating hand and foot point unerringly in the direction of the target. The spread of the stretching arms (almost exaggeratedly long, for effect?) and the legs, with the weight of the body balanced on the heel of one foot and the ball of the other, imparts godlike energy, dynamism and purpose. The massive torso, without any contortion or strain in the evenly balanced musculature, gives the statue a calm assurance and dignified poise. There is a stylised beauty in the hair with its plaited wreath and hyacinthine fringe, and in the beard with its regular sweeping curls. The sharp angle of the beard when viewed in profile is a masterly touch (imagine the figure either unbearded or with the beard flowing down), accentuating the jutting jawline of the god, pointing towards the target, and intensifying the sense of purpose and power which the sculptor has imparted to the bronze.

Equally assured is the *diskobolos* (discus-thrower) of Myron (*c.* 460–450). Unlike the Apollo or the Poseidon, this is not known in the original but through several Roman copies, for the poise and balance of its dynamic pose were celebrated in the ancient world. With the *diskobolos*, sculpture is fully liberated from the restrictions of archaic forms. The original was in bronze, a more flexible medium, and did not need the support of the tree trunk provided for the heavier marble copy (fig. 26). The figure is harmoniously proportioned and represents the ideal male athlete in a moment of arrested motion. So ideal is it, that it is disputed whether the body can actually attain the poise of this pose. Despite the crease at the waist, the muscles of the torso are not responsive to the movement of the arms: there is no sign of muscular strain. The general balance is achieved by answering curves. The delicate positioning of the head, the lower hand and the rear foot contribute greatly to the final poise.

High classicism

Art historians call the style of the early classical sculpture (*c.* 480–450) severe in contrast to the more rounded and fully three-dimensional art that followed. The *diskobolos*, for example, is largely two-dimensional, allowing no proper view from the sides. Although the straight lines of Apollo's body make a deliberate contrast with the other figures in the Olympian pediment and are fully naturalistic, the pose is more rigid than is usual in the developed classical style from about 450 onwards, the great masters of which are the Athenian Pheidias and the Argive Polyclitus.

There are more than thirty copies of the most well-known statue by Polyclitus, the *doryphoros* or spear-bearer (fig. 29), testifying to its fame in antiquity. The original was in bronze and so did not need the prop provided for the marble copy. The figure, sometimes identified as Achilles, carries the spear in his left hand so that the left shoulder is slightly raised. The line of the shoulders is no longer horizontal as it is in the Critian boy

Figure 26 Myron: *diskobolos* (Rome: Terme)

Figure 27　God of Artemisium (Athens: National Museum)

Figure 28　Detail of the
God of Artemisium

Figure 29   Polyclitus: *doryphoros* (Naples: National Museum)

(fig. 24b). In fact the freedom and flexibility have been greatly advanced. Polyclitus has captured a moment of pause in an attitude that expresses movement, whether the figure is imagined to be coming to a halt or starting to walk. The asymmetrical balance of the limbs achieved in the Critian boy is now more fully developed and combined with a torso that is more fully responsive to the tilt of the hips in what is the developed 'contraposto' pose. Artists of the Renaissance admired this pose in the Apollo Belvedere, a Hellenistic statue discovered in 1506, the fame and reputation of which were eclipsed with the discovery of the Elgin marbles when they were exhibited in London in the early years of the nineteenth century. The turn of the spear-bearer's head completes the rhythm of the statue, making an S curve (imagine the effect if the head were straightened or turned the other way). The flexible pose allows pleasing views from the sides, so that the figure is more fully rounded.

The statue was famous doubtless for its beauty, but also because it was known to be the embodiment of the consciously conceived idea of proportion that Polyclitus set out in a book called the *Canon*. Because of this, Pliny tells us, the statue itself was called the Canon:

> He made also the statue that sculptors call the Canon, from which they derive art's precepts as though from a code of law; for he, alone of mankind, is deemed to have put Art's very self into a work of Art.
>
> (*Natural History*, XXIV, 55)

The book does not survive, but from accounts of it and quotations in other authors it is clear that the sculptor thought the secret of beauty to lie in commensurability of the parts:

> of finger to finger, and of all the fingers to the palm and the wrist, and of these to the forearm and of the forearm to the upper arm and of all the parts to each other. [cited by the medical writer Galen (AD *c*. 129–99)] He said that the employment of a great many numbers would *almost* engender perfection in sculpture. [cited by Philo (*c*. 30 BC–AD *c*. 45)]

Perhaps Polyclitus, like Plato and others, was influenced by the Pythagorean doctrine that number is the ultimate reality.

Figure 30 Bust of Pericles (London: British Museum, Townley Collection)

Though the actual basis of the theory has never been satisfactorily explained, and though it seems clear from his modifying use of 'almost' that Polyclitus believed that perfection could not wholly be engendered by the determination of optimum ratios, the Canon bears witness to the Greek belief in due measure in all things, to the Greek principle that art is subject to the rule of reason and to the Greek quest for the ideal form manifested in the art of the fifth century before it became the preoccupation of philosophy in the fourth.

The ancients regarded Pheidias, whom they called the maker of gods, as their greatest sculptor. Regrettably, none of his many works survives. His most famous were the great cult statues, decorated in ivory and gold, of Athene made for the Parthenon and of Zeus made for the temple at Olympia (built earlier in the 460s). The Olympian Zeus, which was enormous (perhaps 40 feet high), was one of the seven wonders of the ancient world. Pheidias is reported to have said that he formed the conception for this most celebrated image from the majestic description of the nod of Zeus in Homer expressing his absolute will: 'Zeus spoke and nodded his dark brow, and the ambrosial locks waved from the king's immortal head, and made great Olympus shake' (*Iliad*, I, 528–30). From ancient accounts, his Zeus is indeed represented in the Homeric attitude enthroned in majesty with a slight inclination of the head and arch of the eyebrows and with the hair gently rolling forward. All accounts agree on the grandeur and beauty of this image which, though awesome, expressed and inspired a benign and detached serenity and did not, like some Byzantine representations of the Christian god, evoke fear. The Roman Quintilian writes: '[its] beauty is

such that it said to have added something even to the awe with
which the god was already regarded: so perfectly did the majesty
of the work give the impression of godhead' (*Education of the
Orator*, XII, 10, 9). Cicero reports that Pheidias did not fashion
his Zeus after any single man but said that there had been in his
mind some perfect picture of beauty which he had contemplated, with which he entirely filled himself and which had
directed his hand. This image, he says, is nothing other than
the Platonic idea of which Plato says that 'it has no birth but is
ever existing and rests in the human reason and understanding'
(*Orator*, 2, 9).

The idealism of classical sculpture can be further illustrated in
the Roman copy (fig. 30) of an Athenian original of about 440 by
Cresilas, 'the Olympian Pericles, a figure worthy of its title',
according to Pliny who adds, 'indeed it is a marvellous thing
about the art of sculpture that it has made noble figures more
noble' (*Natural History*, XXXIV, 74). Pericles was nicknamed the
Olympian perhaps because of his aloofness, his thundering
oratory or his high and mighty ways. According to Plutarch,
the Athenian comic poets also called him *schinokephalos*, squill-
head, because of the shape of his head (*Life of Pericles*, 3). The
helmet therefore has a dual function: to express the dignity of his
position as general (political and military leadership usually went
together in fifth-century Athens) and also to disguise the onion
shape of his head. However near or far it may be from the actual
features of Pericles, the severe and dignified image represents
him as the philosopher-general of Athens and as such expresses
the idealism of the Periclean age. Generally speaking, realistic
portraiture did not develop until the Hellenistic period.

Equally ideal is the head of one of the chariot horses of Selene,
the moon, from the east pediment of the Parthenon (fig. 31). The
eyes, the nostril and the mouth, together with the tautness of the
sinewy nose and the muscular neck, are beautifully naturalistic,
yet the overall effect is to suggest a powerful and epic nobility
that is almost beyond nature. The artist may be said to have
encapsulated the essence of the equine, the Platonic form of a
horse's head, or at the very least to have sculpted a horse worthy
of a god.

The sculptors of the Parthenon are not known, but are
thought to have been a team under the direction of a single
hand and mind, probably of Pheidias. The metope showing a

ART

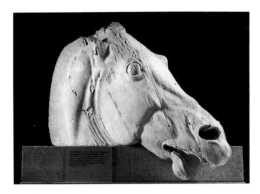

Figure 31 Horse of Selene (London: British Museum)

Figure 32 Lapith and Centaur (London: British Museum)

190

Figure 33   Deities from the Parthenon frieze (London: British Museum)

Lapith in single combat with a Centaur (fig. 32) is finely composed and executed. The dynamic positioning of the Lapith's legs and the contrasting lines of the stretched torsos create a composition of vivid energy for which the sweeping curves of the Lapith's cloak provide a dramatic backcloth. The variously folded drapery which is less solid than that of the previous age (compare the Olympian Apollo, fig. 25), also adds depth; in the centre are three layers represented by the cloak, the Centaur's flank and the Lapith's leg.

The three seated figures from the Parthenon frieze (fig. 33) are identified as Poseidon, and the twins Apollo and Artemis. Again, in the arrangement of the three seats is the illusion of depth. The three figures are relaxed in a pleasing variety of poses. Here the clinging drapery is used to suggest the forms of the body underneath. Like the Muse of the Achilles–painter (fig. 20), the graceful figures are all calm and passionless in expression, yet they are nevertheless endued with life. Serenity is conveyed through the attitude and composure of the whole body.

In the figure from the west pediment, identified as Iris (fig. 34), the clinging drapery not only suggests the form of the bosom, the

Figure 34   Iris from the Parthenon pediment (London: British Museum)

belly and the thighs, but also in the direction of its finely carved curves give the strong impression of movement appropriate to a figure who was the messenger of the gods. The use of drapery to enhance form and to suggest movement in a three-dimensional composition is one of the many techniques perfected in the classical period.

Fourth-century sculpture

The greatest master of later sculpture is the Athenian Praxiteles who flourished in the mid-fourth century. The Hermes with the infant Dionysus (fig. 35), discovered in 1877, is usually thought to

Figure 35   Praxiteles: Hermes (London: British Museum)

be an original by him and, if so, is one of the few free-standing statues to have survived from the classical period. It is thought that the missing right arm dangled a bunch of grapes to which the infant makes a forward gesture. Its beauty is softer and more delicately sensuous than that of anything discussed so far, and in the small head and long legs Praxiteles has his own canon of proportion that differs from that of the stockier figure of Polyclitus. The Hermes also has more fluid lines than the *doryphoros*. It is often said that while the sculptors of the fifth century made gods of men, those of the fourth made men of gods. Yet this image of Hermes has majesty – the body has strength as well as grace – and the Homeric description of Hermes emphasises his youthful charm (see p. 25). However, the soft dreaminess of the face is certainly far removed from the severity of the Olympian Apollo (fig. 25).

The Hermes was not particularly famous in antiquity, but Praxiteles was the author of what, after the Zeus of Pheidias, was the most famous statue in the ancient world, the Cnidian Aphrodite. Pliny tells us that Praxiteles made and sold together two statues of the goddess, one draped and for this reason preferred by the people of Cos while the other, which they had refused, was wholly nude and bought by the people of Cnidos. When later an offer was made to purchase the statue for the price of their national debt, the Cnidians refused, for the statue was their main claim to fame. Pliny goes on to say that the shrine in which it was displayed was entirely open so that it could be viewed from any angle, from which it was equally admirable (*Natural History*, XXXVI, 20–2). The original does not survive but it was much copied by the Romans (see fig. 36). In a modest pose, Aphrodite is about to take a bath. As in the case of Hermes, there is a fine contrast between the intricate drapery and the smoothness of the body (Praxiteles is noted for the softness of his modelling). In addition to the obvious charms of the curvaceous body, a later admirer of the original, Lucian, of the second century AD, comments on 'the liquid gaze of the eye, so clear and full of charm' (*The Art of Portraiture*, 6), a characteristic not apparent in the cruder Roman copy. When Praxiteles was asked which of his own works in marble he placed the

Figure 36   Praxiteles: Aphrodite (Rome: Vatican)

highest, he replied: 'The ones to which Nicias has set his hand',
according to Pliny who adds 'so much value did he assign to his
colouring of surfaces' (*Natural History*, **XXXV**, 133). The Cnidian
Aphrodite, like other Greek statues, owed its effect partly to the
touch of the painter, a point which it is difficult for the modern
onlooker to appreciate, accustomed as we are to the plain white
surface of the marble. More famous in the modern world is the
Aphrodite from Melos (the Venus de Milo) (fig. 37), named after
the island where it was discovered in 1820. The swirling figure of
this fine statue (which dates from the second century) is draped
from the hips to the feet. The pose has less natural poise than
that of her Cnidian counterpart, but the grave beauty of her
handsome head with its confident gaze reflects something of the
serenity of the classical models from which her sculptor doubtless
worked.

The late antique

Finally, as a counterpoint to the classic may be juxtaposed what
has often been called the baroque style of one of the most
famous sculptures to survive antiquity, the Laocoon (fig. 38),
thought by Pliny to be a work superior to any painting or
bronze and assigned by him to the Rhodian sculptors, Hagesan-
der, Polydorus and Athenodorus (*Natural History*, **XXXVI**, 37).
There has been some debate about its date but scholars of art
are agreed on the essentially Hellenistic inspiration of its style. A
dramatic struggle is being enacted in three stages. The two sons
are used to intensify the struggle, centred upon Laocoon, by
showing its beginning and its outcome. The elder son, who is
slightly detached from the other two figures (for he has only just
been caught in the coils of the snake), sees his fate in the still
struggling father at the centre and in his younger brother, whose
limply swooning body has been virtually overcome. The inevitability of the outcome is finely suggested by the arrangement of
the sequence in reverse order (from left to right), starting with
the final yielding swoon, and also by the inclination of the body
of Laocoon towards his swooning younger son. Anguish is
expressed in the different attitudes of the three figures, and the

Figure 37 Aphrodite from Melos (Paris: Louvre)

Figure 38 Laocoon (Rome: Vatican)

agonising toil is communicated through the contorted muscles and swelling veins of the swirling figure of Laocoon, whose arm muscles may be said to reflect the intricate coils of the snake and whose hair and beard are also noticeably snaky.

Although the immediate impression made by this complex structure is one of cluttered intricacy, it cannot be doubted that there is unity if not simplicity of design. Classical clarity of design, simple economy of line and restraint of form have been sacrificed to obtain maximum pathos. For the dramatic emotion that it evokes is the statue's whole reason for being and not any preoccupation with ideal beauty or perfect physical form. Even in battle scenes the classical sculptor preserves the beauty of bodily forms. The dynamic Lapith (fig. 32) retains a grace in action; the muscles of the thighs and arms are taut but not contorted, the chest is uplifted slightly but not twisted. There is a simple beauty in the positioning of the legs as he is poised for action. It is as if the scene has been designed to exhibit an athletic aspect of the body's beauty. This accounts for its uplift-ing effect, what has been called the calm grandeur of high classicism. The uplifting effect is achieved by artistic restraint and emotional detachment on the part of the sculptor, who is intent solely on exhibiting his mastery of the medium and control of form. The artists of the Laocoon, by contrast, have designs on our emotions, and it is the remarkable emotional intensity of the group shown in anguished expression and con-torted forms that sets it apart from the serenity and poise of classical art.

APPENDIX 1
CHRONOLOGICAL TABLE

This is confined for the most part to events and works given significant mention in this book. Fuller versions can be found in *The Oxford Companion to Classical Literature* and *The Oxford History of the Classical World*. Before about 550 most dates are approximate. The abbreviation *fl.* for *floruit* or *floruerunt* (he/she/it/they flourished) represents a scholarly estimate in the absence of firm knowledge.

HISTORY AND EVENTS	CULTURAL RECORD

BC

Bronze Age

3000–1000 Minoan civilisation	
1400 Destruction of Cnossos	
1580–1120 Mycenaean civilisation	
1250 Destruction of Troy	

Iron Age – Dark Age

1100 Dorian invasions Colonisation of Asia Minor	
	875–750 Geometric pottery
776 The first Olympiad	750 Greek alphabet on Phoenician model
	750 Homer
	c. 720 Dipylon vase

Archaic period

730–710 Sparta conquers
Messenia

725 First stone temple at
Sparta
720–620 Orientalising period
in pottery
700 Hesiod
650 Development of 650 Archilochus *fl.*
'Lycurgan' constitution at
Sparta

630 First marble *kouros*

620 Draconian code at Athens

610 Sappho, Alcaeus *fl.* Attic
black-figure pottery begins
600 Thales of Miletus (first
Ionian philosopher)

594 Archonship of Solon
561 First rule of Peisistratus
546 Persian King Cyrus
defeats Croesus of Lydia
545–510 Tyranny of the
Peisistratids
Reorganisation of the
Panathenaea
Institution of the state
Dionysia

535 Thespis *fl.*
530 Pythagoras *fl.* Exekias,
potter and painter *fl.*
Development of red-figure
technique

510 Expulsion of Peisistratids
508 Democratic reforms of
Cleisthenes

500 Heraclitus of Ephesus *fl.*

499 Revolt of Ionian states
against Persia
498 Burning of Sardis 498 Earliest surviving poem of
Pindar

494 Ionian revolt subdued
490–479 Persian Wars

HISTORY AND EVENTS	CULTURAL RECORD

490 Invasion of Darius Battle of Marathon	490 Parmenides of Elea *fl.* Critian *kouros*
487 Ostracism first used	487 First comedy performed at Dionysia
	484 First victory of Aeschylus (b. *c.* 525)
480 Xerxes invades Greece Battle of Salamis	

Classical Period

478 Delian League formed	
	475–447 Polygnotus the painter active Niobid-painter
	472 Aeschylus: *Persians*
	470–30 Career of sculptor Myron (*diskobolos*)
	469 Socrates born
	468 First victory of Sophocles (b. *c.* 496) over Aeschylus
462/1 Democratic reforms of Ephialtes and Pericles	
461–429 Ascendancy of Pericles	
461–456 Building of Long Walls from Athens to Piraeus	
	460–420 Careers of sculptors Polyclitus and Pheidias
	458 Aeschylus: *Oresteia*
	456 Death of Aeschylus Completion of the temple of Zeus at Olympia
	455 First play by Euripides (b. *c.* 485)
454 Treasury of Delian League moved to Athens	

	c. 450 Temple of Poseidon at Paestum
449 Peace of Callias between Athens and Persia	
447 Pericles calls Panhellenic congress	447 Parthenon begun
446 Thirty Years Peace between Athens and Sparta	446 Pindar's last ode
	c. 441 Sophocles: *Antigone*
	c. 435 Herodotus: *Histories* (b. *c.* 484) Achilles-painter
	432 Parthenon completed
431–404 Peloponnesian War	431 Thucydides (b. *c.* 460) begins his history Europides: *Medea*
430 Plague at Athens	430 Hippocrates of Cos (medicine), Protagoras of Abdera (sophist), Zeuxis of Heraclea and Parrhasius of Ephesus (painters) *fl.*
429 Death of Pericles (b. *c.* 495)	*c.* 429 Sophocles: *King Oedipus*
	427 Georgias of Leontini (rhetorician) at Athens Plato born
	424 Aristophanes (b. *c.* 445): *Knights*
	423 Aristophanes: *Clouds*
421 Peace of Nicias	
415–413 Sicilian expedition	
411 Oligarchic revolution	411 Aristophanes: *Thesmophoriazusae*
410 Restoration of democracy	
	406 Deaths of Sophocles and Euripides
405 Battle of Aegospotami	405 Aristophanes: *Frogs* Performance of *Bacchae* of Euripides
404 Defeat of Athens Spartan supremacy	
	c. 400 Thucydides: *History of the Peloponnesian War*
399 Trial of Socrates	
	c. 392 Aristophanes: *Assemblywomen*

HISTORY AND EVENTS	CULTURAL RECORD
	390–354 Xenophon active
387/6 The King's Peace	387 Plato founds the Academy
	384 Aristotle and Demosthenes born
	380 Isocrates (b. 436): *Panegyricus*
	c. 380 Plato: *Republic*, *Symposium*
377 Second Athenian League	
371 Battle of Leuctra: eclipse of Spartan power	
	370–330 Praxiteles (sculptor) active
	367 Aristotle attends Plato's Academy
	360–325 Diogenes the cynic active
359 Accession of Philip II of Macedon (b. *c.* 383)	
357 Philip takes Amphipolis	
355 Collapse of Second Athenian League	
	351 Demosthenes: *Philippic I*
	350–320 Apelles (painter) active
349 Philip threatens Chalcidice	349 Demosthenes: *Olynthiacs*
348 Philip captures Olynthus	
346 Peace of Callicrates	346 Isocrates: *Philip* Demosthenes: *On the Peace*
	344 Demosthenes: *Philippic II*
342 Philip in Thrace	342 Demosthenes: *Philippic III*, *On the Chersonese*
338 Philip defeats Greeks at battle of Chaeronea	338 Death of Isocrates
337 Philip calls Panhellenic congress at Corinth	
336 Assassination of Philip	
	335 Aristotle founds the Lyceum: *Nicomachean Ethics*, *Poetics*

336–323	Career of Alexander the Great (b. 356)		
334	Alexander in Asia		
333	Battle of Issus		
331	Foundation of Alexandria		
331	Battle of Gaugamela		
		330	Demosthenes: *On the Crown*
327	Alexander in India		
323	Death of Alexander		
322	Revolt of Greeks. Battle of Crannon. End of democracy at Athens	322	Deaths of Aristotle and Demosthenes

Hellenistic period

316	Menander (b. 342): *Dyskolos*
307	Epicurus founds school at Athens
300	Zeno of Citium establishes Stoic school on *Stoa Poikile* at Athens Euclid (mathematician) active
270	Aratus, Callimachus and Theocritus *fl.*
262	Cleanthes succeeds Zeno as head of Stoics
c. 260	Apollonius of Rhodes: *Argonautica*
260–212	Archimedes active

Roman period

197	The Romans defeat Philip V of Macedon at Cynoscephalae		
		180	Aristarchus heads Alexandrian library
146	The Romans destroy Corinth: Greece becomes a Roman protectorate		

HISTORY AND EVENTS	**CULTURAL RECORD**
	30 Dionysius of Halicarnassus active at Rome

AD

23/4–79	Pliny the Elder, Latin writer on Greek art
c. 46–120	Plutarch: *Parallel Lives* *On the Sublime* attributed to the rhetorician Longinus
c. 160	Pausanias: *Description of Greece*

APPENDIX 2
LIST OF TRANSLATIONS
CITED IN THE TEXT

In citing modern translations, for the sake of uniformity, Penguin Classics, the most accessible texts, have been used for the most part. Where they are not available, translations from the bilingual Loeb Classical Library have been used. Any translation in the text not cited here is by the present writer.

From Penguin Classics, published by Penguin Books, Harmondsworth:

Author and title	*Translator and date*
Aeschylus: *The Persians,* in *Prometheus Bound and Other Plays*	Philip Vellacott, 1961
Aristophanes: *The Knights, Peace, Wealth*	Alan H. Sommerstein, 1978
Aristotle: *The Ethics*	J. A. K. Thomson, 1953
Aristotle: *On the Art of Poetry* in *Classical Literary Criticism*	T. S. Dorsch, 1965
Aristotle: *Politics*	T. A. Sinclair, 1962
Demosthenes: *Philippics, Olynthiacs On the Chersonese* in *Greek Political Oratory*	A. N. W. Saunders, 1970
Euripides: *Medea and Other Plays*	Philip Vellacott, 1963
Herodotus: *The Histories*	Aubrey de Sélincourt, 1954
Homer: *The Odyssey*	E. V. Rieu, 1946
Isocrates: *Panegyricus, Philip* in *Greek Political Oratory*	A. N. W. Saunders, 1970
Longinus: *On the Sublime* in *Classical Literary Criticism*	T. S. Dorsch, 1965
Lysias: *Against Eratosthenes* in *Greek Political Oratory*	A. N. W. Saunders, 1970

TRANSLATIONS CITED IN TEXT

Author and title	*Translator and date*
Plato: *The Apology* in *The Last Days of Socrates*	Hugh Tredennick and Harold Tarrant, 1993
Plato: *Gorgias*	Walter Hamilton, 1960
Plato: *The Republic*	Desmond Lee, second edition, 1974
Plato: *The Symposium*	Walter Hamilton, 1951
Plutarch: 'Life of Nicias', 'Life of Pericles' in *The Rise and Fall of Athens*	Ian Scott-Kilvert, 1960
Sophocles: *The Theban Plays*	E. F. Watling, 1947
Theocritus: *The Idylls*	Robert Wells, 1989
Thucydides: *History of the Peloponnesian War*	Rex Warner, 1954
Xenophon: *Memoirs of Socrates and The Symposium*	Hugh Tredennick, 1970

From The Loeb Classical Library, published by Heinemann, London and Harvard University Press, Cambridge, Mass.

Author and title	*Translator and date*
Aristotle: *De Anima* (On the Soul)	Hugh Lawson-Tancred, 1986
Aristotle: *Physics*	Philip H. Wicksteed and Francis H. Cornford, 1929
Aristotle: *Metaphysics*	Hugh Tredennick, 1975
Dionysius of Halicarnassus: *The Critical Essays*	Stephen Usher, 1974
Epicurus: in Diogenes Laertius: *Lives of the Eminent Philosophers*	R. D. Hicks, 1925
Pliny: *Natural History*	H. Rackham, 1967

SUGGESTIONS FOR
FURTHER READING

Works of General Reference

Boardman, John, Griffin, Jasper, and Murray, Oswyn (eds), *The Oxford History of the Classical World: Greece and the Hellenistic World*, Oxford University Press, Oxford and New York, 1988.

Cornish, F. W. (ed.), *A Concise Dictionary of Greek and Roman Antiquities*, John Murray, London, 1898.

Grant, Michael and Hazel, John (eds), *Who's Who in Classical Mythology*, Weidenfeld and Nicolson, London and New York, 1979.

Hammond, N. G. L. and Scullard, H. H. (eds), *The Oxford Classical Dictionary*, second edition, Oxford University Press, Oxford and New York, 1970.

Howatson, M. C. (ed.), *The Oxford Companion to Classical Literature*, new edition, Oxford University Press, Oxford and New York, 1989.

McEvedy, Colin (ed.), *The Penquin Atlas of Ancient History*, Penguin, London and New York, 1967.

Rose, H. J., *A Handbook of Classical Mythology*, Methuen, London, 1928 (reissued 1964).

The World of Athens: An Introduction to Classical Athenian Culture, Joint Association of Classical Teachers, Cambridge University Press, Cambridge, 1974.

The Homeric Poems

Finley, M. I., *The World of Odysseus*, Chatto and Windus, London, 1956.

Kirk, G. S., *The Songs of Homer*, Cambridge University Press, Cambridge, 1962.

Griffin, Jasper, *Homer on Life and Death*, Oxford University Press, Oxford and New York, 1980.

Owen, E. T., *The Story of the Iliad*, Bell, London, 1947 (reissued Bristol Classical Press, Bristol, 1989).

Parry, Adam, *The Making of Homeric Verse: Collected Papers of Milman Parry*, Oxford University Press, Oxford and New York, 1970.

Stanford, W. B., *The Ulysses Theme: Studies in the Adaptability of a Traditional Hero*, second edition, Blackwell, Oxford, 1963.

Wace, A. J. B. and Stubbings, F. H. (eds), *A Companion to Homer*, Macmillan, London, 1962

History

Andrewes, A., *Greek Society*, Penguin, Harmondsworth, 1975.

Bury, J. B., *A History of Greece*, fourth edition revised by Russell Meiggs, St Martin's Press, New York, 1975.

Cornford, F. M., *Thucydides Mythistoricus*, Edward Arnold, London, 1907.

Davies, J. K., *Democracy and Classical Greece*, Fontana History of the Ancient World, HarperCollins, London, 1980.

Ehrenberg, Victor, *From Solon to Socrates: Greek History and Civilisation during the 6th and 5th Centuries BC*, Methuen, London, 1973.

Jones, A. H. M., *Athenian Democracy*, Blackwell, Oxford, 1957.

Murray, Oswyn, *Early Greece*, Fontana Library of the Ancient World, HarperCollins, London, 1980.

Walbank, F. W., *The Hellenistic World*, Fontana History of the Ancient World, HarperCollins, London, 1979.

Literature (for Homer, see the earlier section above)

Atkins, J. W. H., *Literary Criticism in Antiquity*, Cambridge University Press, Cambridge, 1934.

Beye, C. R., *Ancient Greek Literature and Society*, second revised edition, Cornell University Press, Ithaca and London, 1987.

Kenney, E. J. and Easterling, P. E. (eds), *The Cambridge History of Classical Literature, I, Greek Literature*, Cambridge University Press, Cambridge, 1985.

Knox, B. M. W., *The Heroic Temper: Studies in Sophoclean Tragedy*, University of California Press, Berkeley, 1966.

Lesky, Albin, *Greek Tragedy* (translated by H. A. Frankfort), Benn, London, Barnes and Noble, New York, 1978.

Mason, H. A., *The Tragic Plane*, Oxford University Press, New York, 1985.

McLeish, Kenneth, *The Theatre of Aristophanes*, Thames and Hudson, London, 1972.

Sandbach, F. H., *The Comic Theatre of Greece and Rome*, Chatto and Windus, London, 1977.

Vickers, Brian, *Towards Greek Tragedy*, Longman, London and New York, 1973.

Philosophy

Cornford, F. M., *Before and After Socrates*, Cambridge University Press, Cambridge, 1932.

Field, G. C., *Plato and his Contempories*, Methuen, London, 1948.

Guthrie, W. K. C., *A History of Greek Philosophy*. 3 vols., Cambridge University Press, Cambridge and New York, 1962–9.

Howie, George, *Aristotle on Education*, Collier-Macmillan, London, Macmillan, New York, 1968.

Hussey, E., *The Presocratics*, Duckworth, London, 1972.

Irwin, Terence, *Classical Thought*, Oxford University Press, Oxford and New York, 1989.

Luce, J. V., *An Introduction to Greek Philosophy*, Thames and Hudson, London, 1993.

Nussbaum, M. C., *The Fragility of Goodness: Luck and Ethics in Greek Tragedy and Philosophy*, Cambridge University Press, Cambridge and New York, 1986.

Ross, W. D. *Aristotle*, Methuen, London, 1923.

Art

Boardman, John, *Greek Art*, new and revised edition, Thames and Hudson, London, 1973.

Carpenter, T. H., *Art and Myth in Ancient Greece*, Thames and Hudson, London, 1991.

Cook, R. M., *Greek Painted Pottery*, Methuen, London, 1972.

Pollitt, J. J., *Art and Experience in Classical Greece*, Cambridge University Press, Cambridge and New York, 1972.

———— *The Art of the Hellenistic Age*, Cambridge University Press, Cambridge and New York, 1986.

Richter, G. M. A., *A Handbook of Greek Art*, sixth edition revised, Phaidon Press, London, 1975.

Robertson, M., *A History of Greek Art*, Cambridge University Press, Cambridge and New York, 1975.

———— *Greek Painting*, Macmillan, London, 1978.

Scherer, Margaret R., *The Legends of Troy in Art and Literature*, Phaidon Press, London, 1969.

Other general works

Bellingham, David, *An Introduction to Greek Mythology*, The Apple Press, London, 1989.

Cameron, Averil and Kuhrt, Amelie (eds), *Images of Women in Antiquity*, revised edition, Routledge, London and New York, 1993.

Clayton, Peter A. and Price, Martin J. (eds), *The Seven Wonders of the Ancient World*, Routledge, London and New York, 1988.

Dodds, E. R., *The Greeks and the Irrational*, University of California Press, Berkeley, 1957.

Dowden, Ken, *The Uses of Greek Mythology*, Approaching the Ancient World, Routledge, London and New York, 1992.
Lacey, W. K., *The Family in Classical Greece*, Thames and Hudson, London, 1968.
Pfeiffer, R., *A History of Classical Scholarship: From the Beginnings to the End of the Hellenistic Age*, Oxford University Press, Oxford and New York, 1958.
Schroder, R. V., *Ancient Greece from the Air*, Thames and Hudson, London, 1974.

The transmission and survival of the Greek legacy

Bolgar, R. R., *The Classical Heritage and its Beneficiaries*, Cambridge University Press, Cambridge and New York, 1954.
Carlsen, H., *A Bibliography of the Classical Tradition in English Literature*, University of Copenhagen Press, Copenhagen, 1985.
Clark, M. L., *Classical Education in Britain 1500–1900*, Cambridge University Press, Cambridge and New York, 1959.
Finley, M. I. (ed.), *The Legacy of Greece: A New Appraisal*, Oxford University Press, Oxford and New York, 1981.
Greenhalgh, Michael, *The Classical Tradition in Art*, Duckworth, London, 1978.
Highet, Gilbert, *The Classical Tradition: Greek and Roman Influences on Western Literature*, Oxford University Press, New York and London, 1949.
Kenney, E. J., *The Classical Text: Aspects of Editing in the Age of the Printed Book*, University of California Press, Berkeley, 1974.
Ogilvie, R. M., *Latin and Greek: A History of the Influence of the Classics on English Life from 1600 to 1918*, Routledge and Kegan Paul, London 1964.
Pfeiffer, R., *A History of Classical Scholarship from 1300 to 1850*, Oxford University Press, Oxford and New York, 1976.
Reynolds, L. D. and Wilson, N. G., *Scribes and Scholars: A Guide to the Transmission of Texts*, second edition, Oxford University Press, Oxford and New York, 1974.
Wind, E., *Pagan Mysteries in the Renaissance*, Faber and Faber, London, 1958.

INDEX

Academy 129, 138
Achilles-painter 165–8, 191
Aeschines 70
Aeschylus 44, 78–9, 81, 82, 83–8, 90, 96, 97–8, 103–4; character in Aristophanes 103–4; **Works**: *Oresteia* 78, 81, 82, 85–8, 90, 96, 97–8; *Persians* 44, 83, 104
agora 23, 30, 34, 48, 50, 78, 102
Alcaeus 74–6
Alcibiades 54–6, 126–7
Alexander 66, 71–2, 138, 165
Alexandrian age 115–17
Anaxagoras 51
Antisthenes 146
Apelles 165
Aphrodite: of Cnidos 194–5; of Melos 195
Apollodorus 163
Apollonius of Rhodes 117
aporia 122, 133
Aquinas 149
Aratus 115
Archilochus 74
Archimedes 149
architecture 51, 168–76
archons 31, 49, 79
Areopagus 31, 32, 49, 83, 87
Aristarchus of Samos 149
Aristarchus of Samothrace 117
Aristides 40, 47, 69, 113
Aristophanes 95, 99–106, 124, 130, 134; Socrates on 125; in *Symposium* 130; **Works**:

Assemblywomen 100, 103, 106, 134; *Birds* 100; *Clouds* 124; *Frogs* 103–6; *Knights* 101–3, 105; *Lysistrata* 100; *Thesmophoriazusae* (*The Poet and the Women*) 95, 129; *Wasps* 100
Aristotle 1, 13–15, 31–2, 66, 90–4, 97, 107, 126, 137–45, 149; on art 145, 150, 164–5; on causes 141; complex plots 91; definition of tragedy 94; difference from Plato 139–40, 145; ideal state 29, 140; on *katharsis* 91, 94; the mean 143–4; *mimesis* 73, 94; parts of tragedy 13, 91; poetry and history 59; tragic fall 92–3; unity of action 1, 13; unmoved mover 141–2; **Works**: *Ethics* 142–5; *History of Animals* 139; *Metaphysics* 118, 138; *On the Soul* 140; *Physics* 138, 141–2, 150, 164; *Poetics* 1, 13–14, 15, 59, 73, 78, 81, 90–4, 97, 99; *Politics* 29, 139–40, 144, 145; *Rhetoric* 115
Asia Minor, Asiatic Greeks 5, 36–8, 40, 41, 55, 63, 64, 71, 72, 74, 118–19
Athens, Athenian (*see also* democracy): architecture 168–76; art 151, 154, 163–4, 168–76, 180, 189–96; character 60–1; Cleisthenes'

213